ADVENTURE
FISHING

ADVENTURE
FISHING

Henry Gilbey

LONDON, NEW YORK, MUNICH,
MELBOURNE, and DELHI

To my wife, Islay, for always standing by me.

Produced for Dorling Kindersley by
Francis Ritter (editorial)
Jo Grey (design)

SENIOR EDITOR
Nicki Lampon

SENIOR ART EDITORS
Anna Benjamin, Alison Shackleton

DTP DESIGNERS
Sonia Charbonnier, Rajen Shah

PRODUCTION CONTROLLER
Mandy Inness

MANAGING EDITORS
Sharon Lucas, Adèle Hayward

MANAGING ART EDITORS
Marianne Markham, Karen Self

CATEGORY PUBLISHER
Stephanie Jackson

ART DIRECTOR
Carole Ash

US EDITORS
Margaret Parrish, Christine Heilman

First American Edition, 2003
03 04 05 06 07 10 9 8 7 6 5 4 3 2 1

Published in the United States by
DK Publishing, Inc.
375 Hudson St
New York, New York 10014

A Cataloging-in-Publication record is available
from the Library of Congress.

US ISBN 0-7894-9341-1

Reproduced by Colourscan, Singapore
Printed and bound in Italy by Canale.

See our complete product line at

www.dk.com

CONTENTS

INTRODUCTION

Before I began this book, almost all of my fishing experience was gained in the rivers, lakes, and coastal waters of Great Britain. Far from seeing that as a limitation or a disadvantage, I now count it as a blessing, for I was able to develop an understanding and true appreciation of the special qualities of the fishing in my own country. Books, magazines, and photographs had made me aware of other fishing destinations, and my mind was filled with those places and their sometimes exotic fish, but somehow the information never challenged my sense of purpose or my sheer enjoyment of fishing, day in, day out, within range of my home.

The lure of adventure

Yet when my publisher inquired whether I would like to travel and gather material for this book, I needed no more than a microsecond of deliberation before giving my very enthusiastic answer in the affirmative. It was a once-in-a-lifetime chance to try some completely unfamiliar fishing, and I knew it was going to be the biggest thrill of my life. Now that the book is completed, I can only hope that my words and pictures will thrill you as much as the actual experiences thrilled me. More important, I hope that you will be inspired to try out some of the different ways of fishing yourself.

While away from home, I came to realize why fishing as a sport offers us all so much. It isn't only a matter of going out and catching fish. I love meeting people who share my interest; I love talking about fishing until my throat goes dry; I shake with pure adrenaline when fishing new places; and I thrive on trying to capture the whole thing, first on camera and then in the written word.

Bigger expectations

My first big trip away was to the desolate Atlantic shore of Namibia, where enormous fish roam no more than a good cast from the beach. Strangely, for two weeks after my return from that extraordinary place, I could see no point in picking up a rod and venturing out to my local spots. The trip had been so good that I seemed to have lost any desire to fish my own grounds. Perhaps it was because no local fish has any hope of attaining the behemoth proportions of the quarry over there. Those feelings intensified when I studied the photographs I had taken and the memories of all those great fish came flooding back.

Then came a phone call: "Henry, a little bit of news; keep it quiet, but there were cod off the headland yesterday. Do you want to make a trip out there tomorrow?" It was my reprieve. The excitement surged back, the adrenaline started to flow, and instantly I packed my cod tackle and went back to what I do and know best. I strode straight down to my favored rock, savoring the pleasures that lay ahead. I had realized once more that fishing is fishing wherever you go, whether your catch is plentiful or not, and the fish tiny and quick or huge and powerful.

Wider experience

If you live in North America, your usual target fish may be salmon, bass, ray, tarpon, or shark; anglers from the European mainland may be more familiar with barbel, pike, or even the mighty wels catfish; my local species include sea bass, thornback ray, pollack, and mullet. As an angler, you grow to love your home species, and traveling need not diminish that feeling. Catching exotic fish is just a way of broadening your experience and making you a better angler.

The angling community

Whether you are fishing far from home or are wetting a line in the local stream, what is it that drives you to do it? Fishing of every kind has a dedicated following, and every angler has a personal reason for taking part. Some anglers dream of hooking record-breaking fish, others dream of fishing from boats, many dream of wandering in absolutely clear water with only lush meadowland or beautiful mountains for company. Whatever your dream, setting out with a rod and reel can make it your reality. My travels also underlined an important factor: that wherever you go, you are almost certain to establish a bond of friendship with your fellow anglers. I know many anglers who take as much pleasure in the cameraderie of fishing as they do in the activity itself.

Like anyone who has fishing in their blood, I have spent many nights lying awake, my mind whirling with images: shore fishing for sharks, mullet fishing in my local estuaries, collecting bait in conditions so cold that my hands turn blue, burning under the Florida sun, and reveling in the worst of English gales as sheets of rain blow in from the Atlantic. Fishing is fishing the world over, yet each time it is different. I hope this book will show just some of the possibilities of fishing in freshwater, from the shore, and out on the open sea.

FRESH WATERS

"We were on tenterhooks, waiting for the bite alarms to sound, or for the splash of hooked fish to ripple across the water..."

The first kind of fishing I ever experienced involved hurling a spinner at some trout in a wild Scottish loch. It therefore seemed right that for the first trip in this chapter, and indeed the whole book, we should stay in Great Britain and go fly-fishing for trout and pike on a beautiful stretch of the Kennet River in England. Although I had previously seen pike in the river, it was amazing to see them caught on a fly. My guide and I compared the manicured, carefully managed banks of the Test and Kennet rivers with the rugged beauty of Exmoor's wilder streams, and looked at the difference between stocked and wild trout. The fishing is different, and I feel very fortunate to have tried both.

My second trip took place on the Baltic coastline of Sweden. I was unprepared for the thriving cult, both Swedish and international, that surrounds fishing for pike in those waters. Innumerable articles on Sweden's "freshwater sharks" had created a growing fascination for them, and I was only too happy to join the cult for a few days and become totally immersed in pike culture. A long-held dream had been to catch a pike of over 10 lb (4.5 kg) on a lure, and I could have done that in no better place, with no better anglers. The place and the fish really are very special.

My third trip was to the Spanish region of Andalusia in the company of the barbel man himself, John Bailey. This was a privilege indeed; John has written a great many books and articles on fishing, particularly on the golden-flanked barbel in our rivers, and I had grown up being inspired by his stories of globetrotting adventures. John was the very person who had unknowingly fed my appetite for fishing as a youngster, so he had to suffer my incessant questions. He also caught the fish as only he can, posed for my camera, and even drove the rental car.

My respect for the man is absolute. While in Andalusia, I recognized that barbel must be among the most visually striking fish that swim in freshwater. I have caught plenty of bigger fish all over the world, but standing in that quietly rippling river, cradling a perfect barbel beneath the hot Spanish sun, is a memory that will stay with me forever.

Off to North America

After Spain we traveled to Florida, a mecca for anglers seeking fish of all kinds. On this occasion my target was the state's world-famous largemouth bass, which inhabit several of Florida's huge and mainly shallow inland waterways. These bass were some of the most voracious and hard-fighting predators I have come across, careering into our livebaits and jumping clear of the water in their attempts to shake the hook. Every dawn on that placid lake was perfect, and nearly every cast produced a fish; what more can the traveling angler ask for?

The next trip was to Canada's Vancouver Island, which was indescribably beautiful. Several species of salmon were running in numbers I would never have believed possible. Catching the salmon was another matter, and it was fantastic to hook truly majestic fish in such perfect scenery. I spent much of my time staring in wonder at both the numbers of fish in the water and the beauty of the rivers. My camera was seldom out of my hands on that Canadian island.

Finally, going after the gigantic wels catfish of the Ebro River was unlike any fishing I had ever done. We were on tenterhooks, waiting for the bite alarms to sound, or for the splash of hooked fish to ripple across the water. Spain is almost nirvana for anglers chasing big catfish, and the people I met on the Ebro banks were at the cutting edge of the sport.

TROUT AND PIKE FISHING IN SOUTH ENGLAND

Trout fishing has always meant something special to me, ever since I caught my first one, guided by my grandmother. Growing older, however, I have come to realize that in Britain the sport exists in various different forms. For example, you can fish for small, wild brown trout in the upland streams of Dartmoor, Exmoor, and many other places in Wales, Scotland, and Ireland. This fishing can be cheap and accessible, and is often found in the most beautiful regions and most challenging terrain of the British countryside.

However, perhaps the best-known trout fishing is the quintessentially English sport taking place on chalk streams, such as the Test, Kennet, and Itchen rivers. Much of this fishing is controlled by private landowners and sports clubs. A premium is usually charged for the privilege of pursuing the brown and rainbow trout in those cherished waters. The rivers are kept in the most beautiful state and the numbers of trout are carefully monitored. Nobody, therefore, could deny that much of the dry-fly fishing there is "manicured" sport. But the chalk streams of England are recognized as the birthplace of modern fly-fishing, and for the angler with a sense of history there is a keen pleasure in fishing those hallowed banks.

"It is possible to lean over every bridge and watch the trout in perfectly clear water..."

The first time I was lucky enough to fish in the pristine waters of the Test River, I was a little too young to appreciate how fortunate I was to be doing it. Now, of course, I know that the cost of a fishing permit there can be very high. But when the invitation came along to relive the experience, I was ready to savor it, and I knew that nothing could be more different from my usual sea fishing.

Experiencing the Test

The Test is a substantial chalk stream, much wider and clearer than the part of the Kennet that had become familiar to me in boyhood. The Test flows in a very hypnotic way, and it is possible to lean over every bridge and watch the trout in perfectly clear water as they move undisturbed around their swims (the areas of water preferred by the fish). Yet should you step too heavily, or break the horizon with your body shape, the fish simply vanish.

BROWN TROUT While the trout that swim in English chalk streams can reach huge proportions, wild specimens are smaller and are often in better condition.

THE ENVIRONMENT

England's chalk streams lie mainly in Hampshire and Dorset and include the Test, Itchen, Frome, Meon, and the Hampshire Avon. The Exe, further west in Devon, flows over sandstone.

Temperatures in England are relatively cool in summer, 59°F (15°C) on average, and mild in winter, 41°F (5°C) on average.

Rainfall and sunshine are intermittent due to rapid successions of weather systems arriving from the Atlantic. Rainfall is high year-round, with rain occurring on average every second day. March and April are the driest months.

Key fish of both the chalk streams and the Exe include brown trout, rainbow trout, and grayling.

Other fish include roach, dace, chub, gudgeon, perch, pike, and eels, with barbel and bream in downstream reaches. The Exe is well-known for flounder, bass, and mullet.

Prime time for trout is generally from May (when the mayfly hatches) until September. The season lasts from March or April to September or October, depending on location. Grayling may be fished until December.

In contrast with sea fishing, much of which is conducted "blind" in the sense that the fish cannot be seen, this form of dry-fly trout fishing consists of seeing rising fish and then casting to them. You must stay quiet, low, and calm, trying to find out which imitation fly the trout will take and where exactly in the flow it is best to try to present it. A trout may well rise, but a bad cast, or an unnatural motion of the fly, and you will never catch a thing.

Stalking the trout

I was fishing that day with David Owen, a very good friend of my family. Absolute patience is the key to this fishing, so David and I wandered up and down the banks, looking for feeding fish. It is always quite magical to see fish rising to feed from the surface, and once you see one the approach must be subtle. Creep nearer the fish, make sure that you have unrestricted space for your back cast, and gently try to offer your chosen fly just upstream of the feeding trout. If you get it just right, your fly will pass naturally over the head of the trout; in a split second, the fish will rise up and seize your imitation. As your line tightens, you strike, hook the trout, and watch as it immediately careers across the river.

The subtle skills of trout fishing are gained over a period of many years. At the end of the morning I had hooked a trout, and was very pleased with my catch, but, meeting David for lunch, I saw that already he had three prime fish. During the afternoon I followed him

with my cameras as he flicked his flies into just the right places with practiced ease. When it comes to this kind of fishing, you are likely to gain as much knowledge from watching a master as you would from practicing alone.

On to the Kennet

My companion on the next stop of my tour of English streams was Nick Hart, a fly-fishing guide and instructor based in Somerset. Our destination was a stretch of the Kennet River, at Ramsbury in Wiltshire, that I had fished many times as a boy. This stretch of the Kennet is not as clear as the Test, but the angler is still looking for rising fish and casting to them. If you stay quiet for long enough, and keep walking quietly up and down the river, you

eventually find a feeding fish. I was reminded that the trout in these Kennet waters always seem to feed in areas where overhanging trees and shrubs make casting very awkward. I watched Nick for a while to see how he approached trout fishing, then set off to find some of my old haunts.

Just around the corner, there was a place that in the past had been very productive for me. I crept up to the water's edge and saw a plump trout sitting in the prime spot. Keeping as low as possible for fear of scaring the trout, I gently put the tiny dry fly ahead of the fish. Nothing, not even a turn of the head. Once again the fly was sent out onto the water and set to drift over the trout's head; this time the fish rose and simply turned away.

RAINBOW TROUT Native to the US, the rainbow trout has been introduced to waters all over the world. It has a very varied diet and has easily adapted to widely differing climates and water conditions.

HIDDEN PREDATOR Lure fishing for pike is one thing; catching it on the fly is quite another. I wanted to know whether my guide, Nick Hart, would succeed on my familiar stretch of the Kennet. I needn't have worried; keeping his distance on the far bank and utilizing his extensive knowledge of pike behavior, Nick tested the water with his fly. He soon landed a beautiful 8-lb (3.5-kg) specimen.

"Suddenly a pike darted out from cover and smashed into the fly like a pit bull terrier..."

Once more the fly line looped out, and this time the fish rose, snatched the fly from the surface, and turned and ran, successfully hooked. The soft rod hooped over and the reel sang as line screeched out. Standing up from my crouched position, I desperately reeled in the line to keep it taut between me and the trout, and thus prevent it from reaching safety. Having averted disaster, I continued to exert the required side strain more and more until the fish was left with no option but to come to hand. I quickly removed the hook, lay on the bank to hold the fish in the water, and let it swim back to its reedy sanctuary.

Pike in the Kennet
Ever since I once saw a huge fish lying close to the bank and motionless, I have known that this part of the Kennet holds pike. Nick is about the most accomplished fly angler that I have ever met and has taken an extraordinary number of species on flies. Once he heard about the pike, he was rigged up in no time.

I had long wanted to see a pike caught on the fly, so I watched with fascination as Nick skillfully placed his fly in likely looking areas. The fly was darting this way and that, just under the surface of the water, when suddenly a pike darted out from cover and smashed into it like a pit bull terrier; it then rushed off around the corner. A pike homes in on safe ground, and this one made every effort to reach sanctuary, but soon enough Nick had the situation under control. He managed to put the net under around 8 lb (3.5 kg) of pike; no monster, true, but a good size from such a narrow stretch of water. "My" piece of the Kennet had suddenly taken on a different,

sinister look, for now everywhere looked as if it might hold pike, ready to dart out and seize its prey. But, once again, a day of fishing had to end; Nick caught the last of his trout, plus a few grayling, and all too soon it was time to break down the rods and head for home.

Brown trout in the Exe
In return, Nick promised to show me how to fish for trout that were completely wild. We drove west to his local Exe River in Devon, where we cast tiny dry flies at the wild brownies. Fishing the Exe costs next to nothing compared to the chalk streams to the east and is one of the purest forms of fishing. These fish have never been stocked and seldom grow large. The angler must stay extremely quiet and crouch down as low as possible; somehow, being totally wild seems to make the fish more likely to scare than ever.

Nick fishes some very tight spots, where casting is no easy task, so I was more than happy just to stand back, watch, and take the photographs. There was no one else out on the moors, and we were able to fish little pools that were alive with wary trout, but we really had to work hard. Nick grew up on this kind of fishing, though, and knows exactly what to do. As I crouched down and tried to keep out of the sight of the fish, eventually Nick caught a few trout. They were small but beautiful specimens, with perfect markings.

Nick would not claim that his fish have great fighting capacities—they struggle to reach 1 lb (0.5 kg). The context of the fishing is more important than the fight, and fishing for trout in the chalk streams and in the Exe could not be more different experiences.

ALTERNATIVE LOCATIONS

New Zealand
If you fish the right rivers, New Zealand has about the finest fly-fishing in the world; big trout, clear waters, and unbelievably beautiful scenery.

Scotland
Here there are hundreds of lochs where you can fish for wild brown trout. The fish tend to be small, but their extreme wariness makes catching them a real challenge. Fabulous fish, great fights, beautiful scenery, cheap fishing, and friendly people.

Montana
Like Scotland, Montana is a region where the angler can fish for wild trout, rather than for fish that have been reared in farms and introduced artificially. And, as in Scotland and New Zealand, you are fishing in magnificent scenery.

TACKLE & TECHNIQUES

River fishing in southern England is done with floating lines. Many anglers are going over to WF (weight forward) line profiles, which aid in long casting, although plenty of people still believe that the more traditional double taper line profile presents flies more effectively. When choosing line, simply match the weight of the line to the weight of the rod. Lines from Rio and Scientific Anglers are recognized as being of fantastic quality; do not buy cheap fly lines because almost invariably they hinder effective casting.

Leaders of 9–12 ft (2.7–3.6 m) in length are ideal for dry-fly fishing in most venues. The knotless, tapered varieties are excellent; a taper down to a breaking strain of 4 lb (1.8 kg) is perfect for chalk streams; for moorland streams, aim for a lighter taper, perhaps down to a breaking strain of 3 lb (1.4 kg).

Dry flies worth trying on the chalk streams are the Gray Duster (10–12), Parachute Adams (12–16), Shadow Mayfly (10), and the CDC F Fly (12–18, in various colors). For the moorland streams, try such patterns as the March Brown (10–14), Black Midge (12–14), CDC F Fly (14–20, in various colors), and the Hairwing Sedge (12–14). Try out any other drab patterns designed to sit in the surface film of the water.

As with all kinds of "lure" fishing, you are trying to trick the fish into taking an imitation of its normal diet. Casting must be accurate and quiet to create a feel of complete normality.

HOME AND DRY *(left)* The moment every angler craves, when the fish is safely in the net.

WILD ONE *(below)* Wild brown trout from the moorlands are smaller than chalk-stream fish.

FLIES

Gray Duster

Parachute Adams

Shadow Mayfly

March Brown

CDC F Fly

Black Midge

Hairwing Sedge

REEL

Lightweight, but strong, construction

Reel feet

Removeable spool

ROD

FLY-FISHING FOR TROUT AND PIKE

Rods In the chalk streams, a fly rod of 8–9 ft (2.4–2.8 m) in 5 weight is good. For moorland streams, a shorter, lighter rod is better, for example 7 ft (2.1 m) in 3 or 4 weights. Top-of-the-line rods are available from Thomas & Thomas, and Sage and Loomis. Tackle companies such as Daiwa and Scierra make excellent fly rods for far less money.

Reels On chalk streams, most anglers prefer disk-drag reels to deal with large fish, although these are less important when targeting smaller fish. Expensive makes include the Orvis Battenkill and the Hardy JLH; cheaper are the ever-reliable Rimfly line from Leeda. Make sure that your reel is balanced with your rod.

TROUT FLIES *(below)* Well-tied flies are designed to imitate the insects that the fish feed upon.

BRIGHT FLIES *(top right)* Some flies are larger or brighter than anything in the natural world.

BROWNIE *(bottom)* This is a typical brown trout from the Exe: small, wild, and difficult to catch.

PIKE FISHING IN SWEDEN'S BALTIC ARCHIPELAGO

Sweden has over 100,000 inland freshwater lakes teeming with fish, including pike and zander. In addition, on the Baltic coast, many huge lakes lie inland of a long archipelago consisting of thousands of tiny islands. The lakes are of brackish water because they are only partly separated from the sea. What is amazing is that abundant monster pike thrive in the essentially salty waters. Fishing for these magnificent predators is a national obsession, and thousands of overseas anglers also make regular pilgrimages to cast lures at them.

Like many visiting anglers, I flew into Stockholm, then drove for two hours southward to Västervik. The town has been open as an angling center for only 15 years; before that, the waters were closed. The place is completely geared to fishing. Everybody seems to fish for pike, and each weekend you see hundreds of boats all over the place, all heading toward their favorite pike haunts. Any angler who values seclusion need not worry; there is so much water around that overcrowding is not a problem. I chose to fish with guides because I am no expert pike angler, but it is just as easy to rent boats and then glean information about the fish from the local angling community.

The day had dawned a little breezy and fairly warm. As I stepped onto just about the most immaculately kept boat I have ever seen, my guide, Anders Forsberg, assured me that conditions looked good for pike. Anders is one of Sweden's best-known angling journalists and, when he is not imparting his extensive knowledge, he is also an excellent guide; there are not many people who know the waters around Västervik better than he does.

To a sunken island

Anders started the quiet four-stroke Honda engine and slowly we made our way to an almost invisible gap between two islands; opening up before us we saw a vast expanse of blue water, trees, and, we hoped, hungry predators. Once we were out into the main bulk of water, Anders opened up the throttle and the boat quite literally leaped up onto the plane and leveled out at around 35 knots.

To the untrained eye, what stretched before us looked nothing more than a lot of water, but with the aid of previous experience and electronics, Anders knew the configuration of the lake bottom. He was after a particular sunken island, over which we would anchor and then cast lures to the pike; the fish are known to hang around these sunken features in order to ambush unsuspecting prey.

NETTING THE QUARRY Pike are big, powerful fish and a net is needed to control them in the last stages of a fight. The net also protects the fish from accidental harm.

"We saw a vast expanse of blue water, trees, and, we hoped, hungry predators..."

THE ENVIRONMENT

Sweden's coast extends for over 1,800 miles (3,000 km), mostly bordering the west of the Baltic Sea. The large pike population at Västervik is sustained by heavy concentrations of prey fish.

Temperatures in the Västervik region average 27°F (–3°C) in January and 64°F (18°C) in July. Temperatures in the far north average 18°F (10°C) colder in winter.

Rainfall and sunshine patterns suggest that the best time to visit is between late May and late July. Summer is partly cloudy; August can be uncomfortably hot and wet.

Key fish in the brackish waters extending inland from Västervik are pike, which grow to over 40 lb (18 kg), and zander, also known as as pike-perch, which prefer a deep, cold-water habitat.

Other fish to be found in the area's inlets include ide (a species of carp), bream, rudd, and roach. Boat fishing for big Atlantic salmon and cod is also available in the Baltic Sea.

Prime time for pike fishing is between late June and early September; the season runs from the beginning of April to the end of October, after which the waters may be frozen. Ice-fishing for pike does occur, but more often in the inland freshwater lakes than the brackish-water Baltic inlets.

ALTERNATIVE LOCATIONS

Canada
A great many Canadians fish for their "muskies" (muskellunge pike) and northern pike; lure fishing is the most popular method. Both of these species are direct relatives of the European pike.

Germany
The gravel pits near Unterfalheim can produce huge pike, and are not heavily fished. The Danube River is also known for pike, as well as the area around the Neckar Valley.

Switzerland
Some of the more remote glacial lakes contain huge pike, 40 lb (18 kg) or more. The fish grow very slowly in the cold water. The chance of locating a good pike is high, but do not expect large numbers of fish.

Scotland and Ireland
The wild lochs of Scotland and Ireland are, for many anglers, the "spiritual" homes of piking. Expect big pike, wild conditions, hard fights, lonely days—and ultimate satisfaction.

"The pike careened this way and that, tail-walking and crash-diving as it tried to shed the hook..."

For 20 minutes nothing happened, and Anders was on the verge of moving off to another mark. But as he went to pull in the anchor, a pike suddenly grabbed my lure less than 6 ft (2 m) from the boat. The light rod immediately took on the most unnatural of shapes and line hissed from the reel as the pike sought sanctuary. I had been casting in the same spot for at least 10 minutes, and the fish must have become so irritated by the rubber lure that it was compelled to follow it to its source and try to kill it. It did not know that the irritating bit of rubber held a hook and a wire trace.

My first big pike
I am not sure whether a little saltwater acts as a performance-enhancing drug to these Swedish pike, but this fish had no intention of showing itself again. It tried every trick in the book to hang deep and smash up the lure, but eventually Anders was able put the net under around 14 lb (6.5 kg) of fish. We were able to admire the perfect mottled markings running down its flanks, and I also had a chance to stare down the most alarmingly armed throat you can imagine. Previously I had only caught a couple of jack pike, so nothing had prepared me for the impressive array of teeth on show. We had no need to kill the magnificent fish, so we unhooked it extremely carefully with a long pair of forceps, and then gently released it back into the depths.

Clearly that fish did not warn its fellows that we were around, for after Anders moved to another sunken island, the pike went on a completely uninhibited feeding frenzy. They seemed to want to lash out at any kind of lure we threw at them. We landed nothing huge that day, considering that the Baltic archipelago has thrown up pike of over 40 lb (18 kg). But I for one had no complaints to make about my first day of serious pike fishing.

Our biggest specimen
The next two days were spent with a young guide named Tobias Storm, and he gave me the choice of fishing either a place that threw up lots of smaller fish, or gambling and going after a better fish. After the previous day's success I had to go for the bigger fish, so we motored up to fish a sunken island that lay between the land and a big, wooded island.

For two days we worked that same spot and managed to pull out a few pike, but on the last afternoon, after having lost a huge specimen, Tobias once again struck into what had to be a decent fish. For 10 minutes he could do little as the pike careened this way and that, tail-walking and crash-diving as it tried desperately to shed the hook. But Tobias is not a guide for nothing. He knew exactly what to do while the pike tried to dictate events, and eventually I was able to slip the net under his fish.

While the pike lay still and stared at me with its unblinking eyes, we both estimated it to be around 20 lb (9 kg). As we returned the awesome, almost prehistoric creature to the water, I gazed one last time upon the biggest pike I had ever seen. This was normal fishing for Tobias and, although he was pleased, he could not quite understand why I was so rapturous in my appreciation. Sometimes just seeing a fish like that is pleasure enough, and it certainly inspires you to strive harder next time to make sure the pike takes your lure.

EXPERT PIKING My guide, Anders, works the rod while his captive pike makes maximum use of the huge, brackish lake as it battles fiercely to escape. Brought to the boat, the pike displays its cavernous predator's mouth. Two beautiful specimens are displayed by my guides, Anders and Tobias (right).

TACKLE & TECHNIQUES

Anglers fishing in the spring look for the deep areas where big females tend to hang around, waiting for the right conditions to spawn. Spring is a good time to catch a real monster because pike feed up before releasing their eggs. As conditions become warmer toward early summer, fishing takes place over underwater islands, many of them lying no deeper than 16 ft (5 m), and in shallow bays and inlets when winds are driving bait fish toward the shore.

On the coast, most of the fishing in Sweden is carried out from boats, so there is no need for any long-distance casting. Boats enable extremely light tackle to be used; only those anglers who fly-fish for pike use lighter gear. When casting lures a short distance

from a boat, braided mainlines come into their own. Anglers let their lures sink to the bottom, and then they either twitch them down there or work them back to the boat. The very positive, nonstretch makeup of braid allows twitching to done more effectively because all the time you can feel exactly how the lure is working. Fighting the pike also has a very positive feel; however, braid has none of the stretch of mono, so you must keep a very close eye on the reel's drag system.

In addition to Sweden's home-manufactured Zalt lure, rubber shads and jelly worms seemed to be most effective. The Swedes fish them on short traces that work best when the lures are "jerked" near the lake bottom.

LATEX LURE (below) Latex shad lures work as well for wreck fishing as they do for piking.

GLITTERING PRIZES (below) A range of pike lures, designed to imitate the predator's prey fish.

LURES

Latex shad lure is effective in both fresh- and saltwater

Treble hook

Diving vane

Jointed body for lifelike movement

FIXED-SPOOL REEL

Adequate line capacity for piking

Corrosion-resistant aluminum body

Fighting drag control

Rear drag

Balanced handle

ROD

LURE FISHING FOR PIKE

Rods My guides favored a very light, one-handed spinning rod. Visiting anglers tended to use special pike rods.

Reels The best lure-casting multipliers are made by ABU and Shimano. Pike anglers should look at the 5000 and 6000 sizes.

Lines Braided mainlines are used in favor of mono.

Traces Wire traces are used to resist the impact of the pike's razor-sharp teeth.

Lures In Sweden the most popular lure, available in a variety of colors, is called the Zalt. The lure is cast and retrieved in a conventional style, unlike the the shads and worms also used.

TODAY'S COLOR *(below)* Yellow succeeded here; lure anglers may pair specific lures with certain conditions.

GLOVED *(below)* Hand protection is wise when bringing pike aboard the boat.

FORCEPS *(below)* Anders uses forceps to unhook a pike.

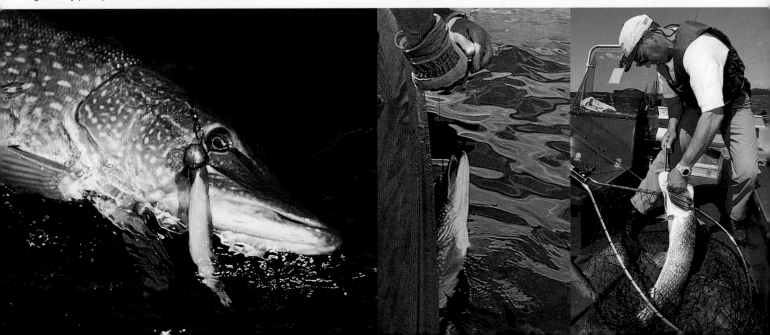

RIVER FISHING FOR SPANISH BARBEL

Up until this trip to Andalusia, in Spain, I had never even wet a line for barbel. It was the most incredible eye-opener; lots of barbel of every size, yet hardly anybody fishes for them. The Spanish varieties are slightly different from their cousins in northern Europe, and the fish are totally wild and absolutely scale-perfect. Andalusian barbel also grow big, reaching weights of over 20 lb (9 kg); most have never been hooked before, and they swim in beautiful waters. In the quiet hills around Andújar we had the chance to use simple, basic methods to catch fish that fight like demons.

Why go to Spain to fish for barbel? Perhaps it was a chance to return to traditional barbel fishing: simple baits, targeting fish that you can see, and fishing in quiet, hidden locations. In northern Europe, the barbel is increasingly pursued in the same way as carp, using a rod-pod, tent, and bite alarm, and with protein-rich baits that make fish huge and overweight. I hoped to find magnificent, golden fish and outwit them in the old way, rather than trick them with special foods and new technology.

Guadalquivir River

Andújar

Córdoba

Seville

ANDALUSIA

Granada

Málaga

SPAIN

"Barbel swam in great numbers in the river's eddies and pools..."

FAST WORK Unhooking a barbel should be done quickly. The species has a relatively low tolerance of spells out of the water and should be returned immediately.

With the hustle of Madrid airport safely behind us, fishing author John Bailey and I headed for the Andalusian town of Andújar, where John knew that a certain river ran full of golden-flanked barbel untroubled by local anglers.

First sight of the river

The Spanish roads seemed empty compared to those at home, and as we drove south the sweeping plains began to give way to hills.

Reaching Andújar, we headed straight for the river. The chance of true Spanish barbel was a temptation too great to resist, especially since this was my first chance to cast bait at them.

My first glimpse of the water was something of an anticlimax; dark gray skies framed a swollen river, and, more importantly, I could see no fish. But John assured me that barbel would still be swimming in great numbers in the river's eddies and pools.

THE ENVIRONMENT

The Guadalquivir River that flows through Andújar, Andalusia, is one of Spain's largest rivers. It collects many smaller tributaries as it flows westward to empty into the Atlantic near Cádiz. John and I were fishing on one of those streams.

Temperatures remain mild in winter, when they average 49°F (9°C). The hottest months are July and August, both averaging 80°F (27°C). The summer heat in the nearby city of Córdoba is second only to that of Seville to the west.

Rainfall and sunshine Summers are typically driest in July and August. Winter rainfall is irregular, with the most rain falling between November and January. Due to its southerly location, most areas of Andalusia experience more than 3,000 hours of sunlight annually.

Key fish in this area of Andalusia include golden barbel, often exceeding 20 lb (9 kg), and carp.

Other fish to be found in the vicinity of Andújar are trout, tench, and pike. The comizo barbel, which can reach 45 lb (20 kg), is found in the Guadiana and Tajo rivers to the north, as are largemouth black bass.

Prime time for pursuing golden barbel is at dusk and in the early morning. The fish do continue to feed in the warmth of the Spanish day but are shy and more difficult to locate.

"Out of the murky water appeared a perfect slab of gold..."

While in Andújar we met Peter Staggs, another barbel fisherman. Together we spent some of the first day laying groundbait, which we hoped would draw the fish to us. Usually the river is almost crystal clear, allowing the fish to be observed easily, but recent heavy rain had colored the water. However, fine weather was forecast for the next few days—good news because the water would regain its clarity.

Beautiful simplicity

John and Peter set up the rods and reels. In all, our approach was very similar to what I might have been doing if estuary fishing for mullet: traveling light, wearing chest or thigh waders, and using simple but effective terminal setups. Generally speaking, I do not oppose bringing advanced technology into fishing, but here that approach would have seemed out of place. Seeing the beauty of the barbel in its natural environment, it seemed obvious that the angler should fish simply, and in a way that caused the minimum of disturbance to the river.

The technique we used was mostly touch-ledger fishing. The weighted bait is cast out to rest on the riverbed, and the taut line is held between the fingers so that any bite is immediately felt. This was very like mullet fishing, so I was not surprised when the first few tap-taps on John's line resulted in a fish. But when John brought his first fish to hand, I could only stand there in admiration. Out of the murky water appeared a perfect slab of gold, twisting and turning all the time. Ready as always to record our fishing, I knew that this species would photograph very well.

ON THE ROCKS Having baited his hook with corn, my guide, the author John Bailey, gently cast the baited trace towards the patrolling fish. When the float disappeared underwater, he knew he had a take. Sure enough, it was not long before a beaming John held his catch, a beautiful golden barbel.

QUIET FISHERMAN Trotting for barbel is one of the more tranquil forms of fishing. Success comes when you blend into your surroundings and give the fish no warning of your presence. John held a catch to show its long whiskers (barbels), which are used in finding food in the riverbed. Our friend, Peter, ensured that the barbel had recovered before letting it slip back into the current.

"You cannot afford to forget that the float is your bite indicator; you must watch it like a hawk..."

To give me a taste of "pure" barbel fishing, John kindly set me up with a "trotting" outfit, comprising a 12-ft (3.6-m) carp-match rod and what is called a center-pin reel. I had heard about center-pin reels, but until then never had a chance to try out such an alien piece of equipment. It was an alarming thing; where was the gearing, or the multiple ball bearings, or the balanced graphite handle? Indeed, I needed John to show me how you actually "cast" the float and bait with this weird reel.

Learning the game

We wandered off downstream to an area we had previously groundbaited with handfuls of corn, and quietly waded out until we could "trot" the float right out into the main flow. The idea of trotting is to cast your hookbait and float upstream, then let them trundle downstream through your groundbait, before reeling them in for another cast. Trotting is not as easy as it sounds. At all times, you must remain focused on your float, your line must be kept tight, and your reactions must be lightning-fast when you sense a take.

Simple float-fishing is something most anglers have done at one time or another. It is always a highly mesmerizing form of fishing; you concentrate solely on your little bit of wood or plastic in the water, upon which rest your hopes for the day's sport. However lost you become in your thoughts or the beauty of your surroundings, you cannot afford to forget that the float is your bite indicator; you must watch it like a hawk.

Letting my float wander off down the river one more time, I struck on impulse at a slight twitch and found an angry fish on my line.

With the spool spinning as the unseen fish sped off, my primary concern was to avoid having my knuckles rapped by the revolving handle. At last mastering the reel, I was able to enjoy the fearsome power of my fish. In no time at all, the barbel raced across the river toward the nearest snag; it only just turned in time as the rod arched over and I held on for dear life, desperately trying to prevent it from reaching sanctuary.

In that fight, all my hopes for barbel fishing came true. Getting my first glimpse of the fish, I nearly forgot I was actually attached to it, so mesmerized was I by the sheer splendor of the fish, the fight, and the breathtaking scenery surrounding us. I kept praying that the hook would hold and the line would not snap, because the barbel's power seemed quite out of proportion to its size. Finally I had it safely to hand and the fight was over. Just how do you define a creature that looks so striking, and yet also blends so perfectly into its environment? The barbel is all that and more.

Protecting the fishing

On our trip, John and I talked for a long time about how he literally grew up fishing for barbel. He firmly believes that fish learn and subsequently can become very wary. So, when you have happened upon "virgin fishing," it is extremely important to fish simply and quietly. That way, you can come back and fish again and again for unspoiled, wild fish in a pristine environment. Go in heavy-handed and the location is never quite the same again. Those of us who love to seek out untouched grounds must temper our joy in fishing new waters with the need to protect what we find.

ALTERNATIVE LOCATIONS

Great Britain
The famous barbel rivers trip off the tongue: the Severn, Trent, Thames, Ouse, Wye, Nid, Kennet, and Ribble. The barbel is becoming a serious cult fish, and anglers are landing some huge specimens, most often with carplike setups.

France
There are large numbers of barbel in some French rivers; look to areas in the south, the Dordogne region, and especially the Lot River, which flows through southwest France. French anglers tend not to target barbel. Much coarse fishing in Europe is done equally for the sport and the table, so perhaps the saving grace of the barbel is that it is not a great eating fish.

Poland, the Czech Republic, and Slovakia
In these countries, barbel can push over the 25-lb (11-kg) mark, but again, poor eating means that they are not much pursued.

TACKLE & TECHNIQUES

Touch-ledger fishing involves casting a simple running ledger or paternoster (a fixed running ledger), with a light weight to keep the bait underwater. The angler watches the rod tip for bites, or, as the technique's name implies, holds the mainline between the fingertips and feels for fish plucks and twitches. Barbel moving into a swim often give you "line bites" as their bodies rub against the mainline, but you must resist the urge to strike until you feel a positive take. Once you decide to strike, you need to respond quickly to set the hook into this clever fish.

Trotting a float requires flow in the water to keep it moving downstream, and it is best to set up the rig so that you are fishing just above the bottom. Float-fishing into slack water and pools works best when you overset the depth slightly, but vary your approach until you start getting bites. If you can see the fish, it is harder to control your impulse to strike; you become convinced that every fish near your floating or weighted bait is taking a nibble on it. Watching a motionless float requires great powers of concentration—it can suddenly twitch and disappear. Then, if you strike too late, you will be striking at nothing.

Above all, do not use a keepnet, because all barbel are easily damaged. Respect the fish; fight them, gently land them, weigh them in a carp sack if you want, and then gently release them.

SIMPLE FARE *(below left)* Perhaps the bright yellow of corn contributes to its success as a bait.

ARTIFICIALS *(below)* Tied flies also work with barbel, which can take food at the surface.

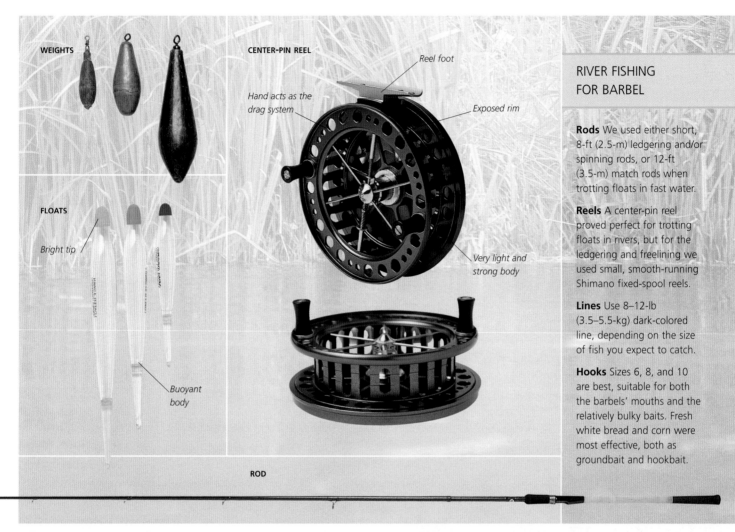

WEIGHTS

FLOATS

Bright tip

Buoyant body

CENTER-PIN REEL

Reel foot

Hand acts as the drag system

Exposed rim

Very light and strong body

ROD

RIVER FISHING FOR BARBEL

Rods We used either short, 8-ft (2.5-m) ledgering and/or spinning rods, or 12-ft (3.5-m) match rods when trotting floats in fast water.

Reels A center-pin reel proved perfect for trotting floats in rivers, but for the ledgering and freelining we used small, smooth-running Shimano fixed-spool reels.

Lines Use 8–12-lb (3.5–5.5-kg) dark-colored line, depending on the size of fish you expect to catch.

Hooks Sizes 6, 8, and 10 are best, suitable for both the barbels' mouths and the relatively bulky baits. Fresh white bread and corn were most effective, both as groundbait and hookbait.

CENTER-PIN REEL *(below)* Mastering this reel is part of the challenge of "simple" barbel fishing.

ALL GOLD *(below)* Somehow, the barbel's flanks of shining gold add to the satisfaction of a catch.

LARGEMOUTH BASS FISHING IN FLORIDA

Just as many European anglers prize the sea bass above all other fish, in the US fishing for largemouth bass is something akin to a religion. An entire economy seems to rest on this somewhat weird-looking fish, with tackle shops, guides, motels, and bait collectors all relying on bass anglers for their income. As in Canada, the fishing is carefully managed to try to ensure that everyone has a satisfying trip and will come again. There is also a "Bass Tour" in which professional anglers make a circuit of several bass-holding states with their boats to win serious money in fishing competitions.

My first largemouth bass trip was to be on Lake Tohopekaliga, not far from Orlando. This large expanse of water is about as perfect as it gets for supporting a huge bass population. Largemouth bass in Florida like to feed hard soon after first light, slowing down as the heat and barometric pressure rise. Fishing can be successful as the day wears on, but many anglers make the most of the beautiful early mornings, setting out onto the lake in the half-light to fish while it is cool and quiet.

"Big mugs of coffee were cradled gingerly as Jamie's boat raced through the maiden-crane grass..."

MONSTER MOUTH
Pike and pollack are equipped with large mouths, but a Florida bass is more like a voracious tunnel that has evolved to engulf its prey.

Racing down to the brightening shore of Lake Tohopekaliga at 6 am, I had no real idea whether it was day or night. Only a few hours of sleep separated me from my flight across the Atlantic to Orlando. It didn't matter; long-distance casting champion Roger Mortimore and I had heard much about largemouth bass fishing, and our guide, Jamie Jackson, had assured us that his local lake was fishing very well—comforting words to traveling anglers.

There can be no better wake-up call than ripping across the glasslike surface of a lake at nearly 60 mph (100 km/h), dressed in only light pants, a T-shirt, and sunscreen. Florida men like to get their fishing fast, and who were we to argue? Big mugs of coffee were cradled gingerly as Jamie's boat raced through the maiden-crane grass and on to our fishing spot.

Beginning at dawn

All thoughts of tiredness and jet lag were quickly forgotten as the boat slowed and came to rest perhaps 33 yd (30 m) from a big grass bed. Over went the anchor as the sun began to peek over the distant trees and the mercury started its inevitable climb.

THE ENVIRONMENT

Lake Tohopekaliga lies south of Orlando and is just one of several vast expanses of water within the state of Florida. With depths of around 10–13 ft (3–4 m), it is the perfect habitat for largemouth bass. Plentiful submerged hydrilla weed is used as cover by the bass, and large shoals of golden shiners and other small fish provide an inexhaustible food supply for the voracious predators.

Temperatures during the summer seem higher than they are because of high humidity. July and August are hottest, with an average maximum of 91°F (33°C). Winters are mild; the average minimum temperature in January (the coolest month) is 48°F (9°C).

Rainfall and sunshine Central Florida has a wet season from May to October, and a dry season from November to April. The hurricane season is from June to November; on average, there are two hurricanes per season.

Key fish in the lake are the largemouth black bass.

Other fish found in Florida lakes include another four bass species: the peacock bass, shoal bass, spotted bass, and Suwannee bass.

Prime time for largemouth bass is between November and March, during the spawning season. Florida peacock bass is best fished from February until May, but all bass species are fished successfully year-round.

"We were hooking leaping fish just one after the other..."

Roger and I had come to the lake at a time of year when largemouth bass fishing is done mainly with live bait. Just as European sea bass are voracious predators, so their freshwater cousins like nothing more than engulfing smaller fish, as many of them as possible. Jamie had picked up a supply of golden shiners from the huge local tackle shop, and they were swimming obliviously in the aerated live-wells, ready for their intended purpose.

As I broke open my camera gear and loaded up with film, Roger cast out bait toward the reeds, and clicked his multiplier into gear. Jamie is a professional bass guide and fishes these waters day in, day out; when he says the bass will feed initially around the maiden-crane grass, it is wise to listen.

Frantic fishing

I had hardly gotten started when Roger swept back his rod, wound down tight, and hooked his first American bass. The fish jumped out of the water, shook its huge mouth, and then tried to run for the sanctuary of the reeds. On Roger's face was a look of sheer delight, and that look was one I often saw among the bass fanatics we met in Florida.

Things soon got really hectic. We were hooking leaping fish just one after the other, and it was like a juggling act trying to work cameras, catch fish, stay calm, and take it all in. It seemed that we could do no wrong, since

PLACID VISTA Fishing in Lake Tohopekaliga was very different from my usual sport in tidal waters. I was easily able to reach for my prize as it reluctantly came to hand. Holding a bass by its bony jaw causes it no harm.

the fish attacked one bait after another. But we knew that, without our guide, we would have had no idea where to look for fish in the huge Lake Toho waterway. Jamie put us on to them, and we were simply reaping the rewards.

Bass fishing is heavily influenced by barometric pressure. Out on the water, Jamie would hold his barometer aloft and study it. As the needle rose and the heat of the day increased, the bass would cease to feed and move out to slightly deeper water. This move to deeper water is said to relieve pressure on the bass's ear bones. For this reason, fishing often takes place early in the morning.

Wrenched from the weed

Early on our second day I hooked a powerful fish that fought with single-minded determination to snag me up in the thick weed. Abandoning any form of subtlety, I had no choice but to lock the reel and try to wrench the fish from its sanctuary. Water cascaded as the bass leaped clear of the water, but the hook held. Jamie slipped the net under my prize, and I was left to admire more than 10 lb (4.5 kg) of largemouth bass.

And that was bass fishing in Florida; take care to slip the fish gently back into the water, crack open an ice-cold drink, pick out another shiner, and then get to it again. Flick the float toward the reeds, tighten up on the line, and be ready to set the hook in that bony mouth. The very rapid ride back to the harbor is just part of the service.

ANOTHER BEAUTY My friend, Roger, levers in a bass while our guide, Jamie, leans out with the net. Jamie then eased out the hook. No one could mistake the predatory nature of this fish.

ALTERNATIVE LOCATIONS

Mexico
Intrepid traveling anglers for largemouth bass are heading for lakes such as Baccarac, Aguamilpa, and El Salto, as well as the Sierra Madre mountains. All contain trophy-sized bass; guides are often available.

Cuba
Fishing in Cuba is not yet developed as a tourist facility. Many waterways are only now being opened up, and there is great potential for largemouth bass fishing.

Texas and California
The larger bass tend to be found in the more southern states of the US. While Florida is the "spiritual" home of the species, thousands of other lakes in the south hold populations of these weird-shaped bass. Professional bass competition tours in the US take in a lot of different lakes and states.

Great Britain
Livebaiting for sea bass is a long-established fishing method off the British coastline. It works because it appeals to the voracious, predatory instinct of the fish. European anglers fish mainly for sea bass (although I have seen largemouth bass caught in Spain), as do the large numbers of Americans who fish for the mighty striped sea bass in US coastal waters.

TACKLE & TECHNIQUES

Using lures to catch largemouth bass is very popular and successful on Lake Tohopekaliga; one look in local anglers' tackle boxes reveals how many varieties of lure will interest this fish. But we were fishing Lake Toho at a time of year when the locals knew livebaiting worked best. When you are fishing away from home, you listen to what the locals say.

Our live baits, called "shiners," were transferred directly from the holding tank of a local tackle shop to the live-wells on Jamie's boat; we never suffered any losses. The baits can be expensive, and you may use a lot of them if the bass are feeding hard, but the quality of the fishing more than justifies the cost.

The shiners were hooked up and fished beneath a very simple float setup.

The secret is to get the bait as near to the grass as possible, in order to present an irresistible meal to the patrolling bass. Jamie anchored the boat as close to the grass as he could without scaring the fish, then made any adjustments to our position using the electric motor.

When the float dips, it is essential to give the fish a little time to take the bait properly. When you strike, you must strike very hard, for these bass have extremely tough mouths. Set the hook, and then bully the fish away from its potential sanctuary in the grass; do all that correctly and the fish is yours.

Largemouth bass are good to eat, but we wanted to return every one. That we did so very easily indicated that they are tough and resilient predators.

BAROMETER (*below left*) Rising barometric pressure causes largemouth bass to cease to feed.

LIVING BAIT (*below*) In Florida live bait is preferred to fishing with lures at certain times of the year.

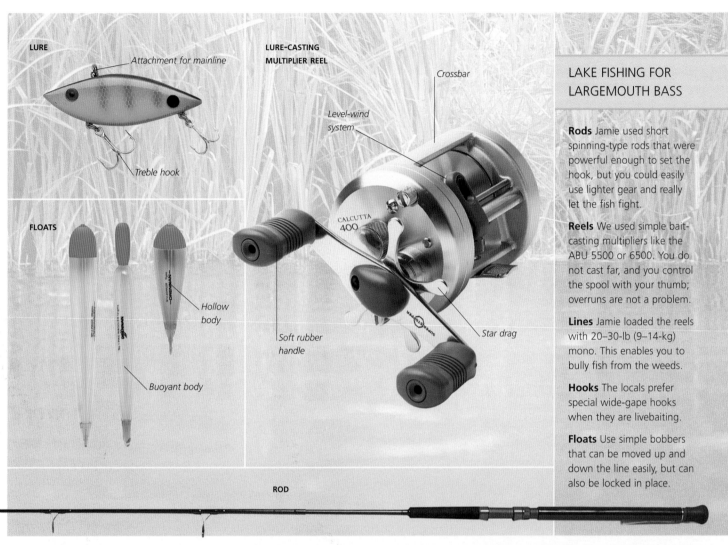

LURE

Attachment for mainline

Treble hook

FLOATS

Hollow body

Buoyant body

LURE-CASTING MULTIPLIER REEL

Crossbar

Level-wind system

CALCUTTA 400

Soft rubber handle

Star drag

ROD

LAKE FISHING FOR LARGEMOUTH BASS

Rods Jamie used short spinning-type rods that were powerful enough to set the hook, but you could easily use lighter gear and really let the fish fight.

Reels We used simple bait-casting multipliers like the ABU 5500 or 6500. You do not cast far, and you control the spool with your thumb; overruns are not a problem.

Lines Jamie loaded the reels with 20–30-lb (9–14-kg) mono. This enables you to bully fish from the weeds.

Hooks The locals prefer special wide-gape hooks when they are livebaiting.

Floats Use simple bobbers that can be moved up and down the line easily, but can also be locked in place.

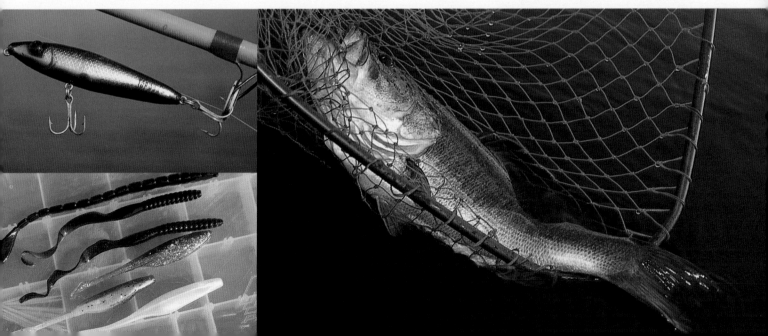

READY FOR ACTION *(below)* This mounted lure is made especially deadly by its two treble hooks.

RUBBER LURES *(bottom left)* Sometimes the wriggle of jelly worms can make them attractive lures.

NETTED BASS *(below)* A landing net is used to get the bigger bass into the boat for unhooking.

SALMON FISHING ON VANCOUVER ISLAND

The sad decline of the great salmon rivers of Scotland and Ireland, attributed to overfarming, offshore commercial pressure, climate changes, and in-river netting, has been an object lesson for the rest of the world. In Canada, Vancouver Island has rivers swarming with salmon species and steelhead trout, and the authorities are determined to keep it so.

After you buy a freshwater license, fishing in the rivers is free, but in return you are expected to adhere to strictly enforced local laws. You do not trifle with the authorities; if they say that you cannot kill certain types of salmon or must avoid fishing certain pools at various times, you obey. Although it is frustrating to see salmon milling around in a pool that has been closed to anglers, everybody has faith that the laws are in the best interests of both the fish and the local fishing economy.

If you want plenty of easily caught salmon, you can go boat fishing, but if you want a real chance to test your patience and skill, then fish the rivers by yourself or with a guide. There are days when the salmon go crazy and jump on the hook, but in general you have to work hard to get your catches on the rivers.

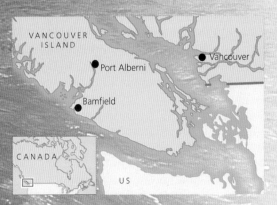

"It was a chance to cast lures into what seemed like virgin pools..."

MALE SALMON This salmon may be identified as a male by its dangerous-looking jaw, known as the kype. A lure is attacked as an annoyance rather than taken as food.

Our base was Bamfield on the southwestern coast of Vancouver Island, a 1½-hour, bone-jangling truck ride from Port Alberni on a logging trail. My first chance to river fish out there came on what was really no more than a big stream, and it was a perfect place to start. My guide, Graeme Pullen, managed to pull a perfect coho salmon out of a pool that I had not even bothered to cast a lure into; I could not believe that a salmon would lie up in a water that small. I was learning fast.

There was one particular river, the Sarita, that for a while ran close to the logging trail and looked very promising. Graeme and I spent one perfect afternoon working our way perhaps 3 miles (5 km) up

the river through deep pools of pristine water surrounded by trees, until we came alongside the road again. We hooked a few small cutthroat trout and lost them, but really it was a chance to cast lures into what seemed like virgin pools. Seeing fresh bear prints on the ground, we were also often looking over our shoulders. After fishing in the river for most of the afternoon, we came to a perfect pool.

"He waded deeper and deeper, trying to control his infuriated fish..."

Rapids were splashing into one end of the pool and Graeme told me that salmon use such fast water to run upriver. The sun was dropping, and this prevented us from seeing into the pool, but we just had to fish it. We began by casting lures across the rippling water, where we could have seen anything moving, but for half an hour there was no sign.

GETTING IN DEEP Vancouver Island's rivers run fast and deep and you need to get into the water to get to most of the salmon runs, or to chase after the fish. My guide, Graeme, could never have hauled in his fish from the bank. His lightweight chest waders and wading boots enabled him to follow his spring salmon and secure it from mid-river. Some hardy men wear only shorts and running shoes in the rivers, but most anglers are grateful for effective insulation from the cold water.

Spring salmon success

Just as I thought I saw something move—it was a huge salmon racing back to the pool—Graeme suddenly hooked another. Together the fish went careening into the black depths of the pool and I ran for my camera, hearing the line screaming from Graeme's reel and the splashing as he waded deeper and deeper, trying to control his infuriated fish. Suddenly his salmon leaped right out of the water, and both of us nearly fell over backward in shock. The power of the fish was remorseless, but sometimes I think a fish is meant to be caught; after about 15 minutes, Graeme had over 20 lb (9 kg) of prime spring salmon lying by him, ready for unhooking. And I am certain that the first salmon I saw was at least double that size. My visit to Canada was certainly challenging all of my preconceptions of salmon.

The next day, we returned and saw perhaps 100 big spring salmon in that pool, but now momentarily trapped by a drop in the water level. Over the following four nerve-shredding hours we could not induce one positive take, but seeing that many fish was unforgettable. A few were certainly around the 40-lb (18-kg) mark, and therefore exceptionally big fish.

THE ENVIRONMENT

Vancouver Island is comparable to a small country in terms of size, with a coastline extending 2,175 miles (3,500 km). The island has 700 lakes, 160 rivers, and 890 streams. Some rivers, such as the Cowichan, Gold, Nitinat, and Stamp, are world-famous for their salmon fishing opportunities.

Temperatures are warmer than on the Canadian mainland due to the moderating effect of the Pacific Ocean, which remains constant at 50°F (10°C). Mildest of all is Victoria, on the island's southern tip, averaging at 65–90°F (18–32°C) in summer and 61°F (16°C) in winter.

Rainfall and sunshine The lowest rainfall is in the south of the island, which has an annual average of 2,183 hours of sunshine.

Key fish in the island's freshwater rivers are the spring salmon, called the chinook or king salmon in the US; Canadians call them tyees when they exceed 30 lb (13.5 kg). Other salmon species include the coho, pink, sockeye, and chum. Trout species include the brown, rainbow, cutthroat, and steelhead.

Other fish found in the freshwater rivers include smallmouth bass and char.

Prime time for spring and coho salmon is August and September, but anglers can switch to other species at other times of the year.

ALTERNATIVE
LOCATIONS

Ireland and Scotland
Fish the famous Irish rivers
and you will almost certainly
catch salmon, although do
not expect a very big
specimen. Many people
happily fish the famous
Scottish salmon rivers. Even
though stocks are lower
than in previous years, you
still have a chance of very
enjoyable fishing; the
scenery is breathtakingly
beautiful, and the people
are extremely friendly.

Russia
While it can be costly to
get to Russia, parts of the
country are reputed to offer
the ultimate in sport fishing.
Only a few companies have
access to the best grounds.
The Kola peninsula is the
place to head for, and it
has real adventure fishing—
there are no restaurants or
hotels, but plenty of fish.

The next day at 3:30 am we were back on the lumpy logging trail and heading in the dark for Port Alberni and the Stamp River. Two guides, Nick Hnennwj and Bladon Zaplotinsky, were going to meet us with their boats and "walk us in," as they call it, enabling us to fish from both bank and boat for salmon and perhaps steelhead trout. As we offloaded our gear from the truck, an amazing sight greeted us; tendrils of mist were rising up from the fast-flowing water and the river seemed to be breathing as it prepared for the influx of salmon from the nearby Barkley Sound. The first rays of day allowed our guides to take the boats out into the middle of the river and drop anchor; we were fishing.

Using yarn lures

John must have had a powerful wake-up call, for on his second cast the lure was snatched by a good spring salmon that ran hard in the racing current. He applied all the pressure he could and still the thing kept running, but eventually the action of the rod had some effect. Soon enough, the shining slab of fresh-run silver was netted, photographed, and gently slipped back to continue its journey.

Moving farther upriver, we started to fish a gravel bar where the river gurgled and ripped over some unseen boulders. Out came our yarn lures and floats, and we cast them out, desperately trying to control their movement in the current. Because salmon do not feed when swimming upriver to spawn, we used yarn lures to "annoy" them into taking the hooks out of inquisitiveness or aggression. I had never fished like this before and was eager for success. I had seen another angler hook a spring so huge that he had to take to the boat with his guide and follow the fish downriver.

The next day, real numbers of salmon were pouring upriver; this was hard fishing, and all

the more fun for being so challenging. I had three good hookups, but every fish shed the barbless hook, including a spring of around 25 lb (11 kg). When this happens, there is not much you can do except hope that next time the struggle will continue until the end.

Surprising power

We were coming to our last hour of fishing. Once more my float was cast well out and upstream, running over a deep pool between big underwater rocks. Shoals of springs and coho were urgently passing us, and Bladon pointed out to me a lone steelhead. Just then my float caught a back eddy and suddenly shot under; instantly I swept the rod back, trying desperately to reel in all the slack line and set the hook at the same time. By this time the float was screaming upriver, barely beneath the surface. As I made proper contact with the fish, it turned and charged downriver into some very fast water; line poured from the little multiplier, but still the hook held. While my forearms began to ache in the most pleasurable of fishing ways, I wondered what on earth I had on the end of the line.

The fish was invisible as it hung perhaps 70 yd (65 m) away in the fast water, so there was no choice but to try a little "bullying" to bring it toward the net. After 10 minutes of concerted pressure, I finally got a first glimpse of my willful adversary. You could say that I was a little shocked, for it was a steelhead barely attaining 9 lb (4 kg), yet still it was fighting extraordinarily hard in the current.

Bladon netted my prize and we duly photographed it, but really I just wanted to see the fish go safely back. It was no monster, but I had done exactly what I wanted to do, which was to conquer an alien method of fishing. Next time I am going after one of those huge springs of over 40 lb (18 kg).

FLY VERSUS LURE While we did try fly-fishing techniques, it was almost impossible to fish flies effectively in the very fast-running and relatively deep waters. The Canadians primarily fish with small lures and yarn, either cast out or fished under special floats. Our salmon were caught on conventional lures.

TACKLE & TECHNIQUES

Many salmon stay near the bottom as they move around their swims. If you are equipped with polarizing sunglasses, they are usually easy to see in the clear Canadian waters. You need to get your lures down as deep as possible to reach the deeper fish. That can be hard when fishing in very fast or deep water, but the effort is worth it; cast out your tackle and let it all sink, and don't be afraid to lose a lure from time to time at the bottom of the river.

The Canadian specialty is to use yarn "lures" suspended under a float, and in the hands of a competent angler this is the most deadly of methods. A piece of brightly colored yarn is simply tied onto a bare hook, weighted down, and then fished under a sliding, foam float. The float can be adjusted easily to fish the yarn at the required depths. I imagined that the yarn would be fished just off the bottom, but was surprised to learn that the float tends to be set considerably deeper than the area being fished. The yarn, or occasionally a small-bladed spinner, is bounced along the bottom, hopefully past the nose of your fish.

Bouncing the lure along the riverbed gives you a lot of false bites as the hook snags on objects, but you have to strike every time in case it really is a fish. The method works best in fast-running water, which imparts a lot of movement to the yarn; if the water is slow, the salmon is more likely to sense that the lure is not worth taking.

CANADIAN YARN (*below left*) Bright yarn is tied onto a bare hook and fished under a float.

BEADS AND FEATHERS (*below*) These lures are simply variations on the Canadian theme.

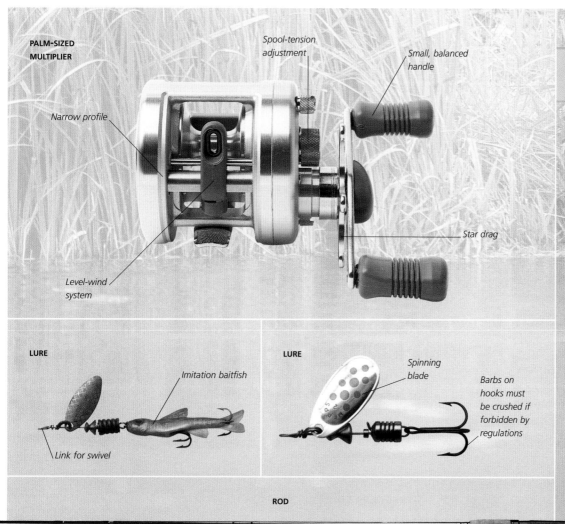

PALM-SIZED MULTIPLIER

Spool-tension adjustment

Small, balanced handle

Narrow profile

Star drag

Level-wind system

LURE

Imitation baitfish

Link for swivel

LURE

Spinning blade

Barbs on hooks must be crushed if forbidden by regulations

ROD

RIVER FISHING FOR SALMON

Rods Most of us tended to use either carp rods or specialized Shimano heavy-duty spinning rods.

Reels We used Shimano or Daiwa fixed-spool reels, such as I use for mullet fishing, but if I did more lure fishing at home I would invest in a selection of Shimano or Abu palm-sized multipliers.

Lines Bearing in mind typical weights of Canadian salmon, I stepped up the line to 20-lb (9-kg) black Ultima F1, which is strong and of a smaller diameter than most.

Swivels Good-quality swivels rotate and help to eliminate line twist when casting lures. Attach a small swivel direct to the lure, then attach that to your mainline via a small link swivel.

UNCONCERNED (below) Salmon tend to ignore food baits when moving to spawning grounds.

SPOONS (bottom left) Salmon and trout are lured by the light bouncing off shiny metal spoons.

THE BOAT OPTION (below) It is sometimes easier to catch fish from a boat than when wading.

CATFISHING ON SPAIN'S EBRO RIVER

Looking down on the Ebro River as it meanders through Catalonia in Spain, you wouldn't think that such an innocent-looking stretch of water could hold a species as large as the catfish. Nobody could claim that the catfish is beautiful, but they do grow to an immense size and there is no finer place to chase them than the Ebro. The river's record for catfish currently stands a little under 200 lb (90 kg), and there are reliable stories of much larger fish lost in the final stages of the battle. I was heading for the stretch closest to Tortosa, which by all accounts is some sort of angling mecca for catfish aficionados.

Unlike sea fishing, where often you must be content with short, sharp sessions when the tides and conditions are favorable, catfishing is a long game and demands extreme patience. It appeals particularly to carp specialists, many of whom think nothing of spending days and weeks at a time fishing their favored swims. Most of the men camped out along the banks of the Ebro are dedicated carp anglers, out in Spain for something considerably larger. But I had only a few days—would I be lucky enough to catch, or at least see, one of these leviathans?

I met up with Dave and Karen McCoy in
Tortosa. Together with Paul Savill, they run a
company that has one main goal: to help their
clients catch catfish. They also guide for other
coarse fish in the Ebro River, such as carp, but
most anglers come to them with only one
thing on their mind, what the Spanish call the
siluro. First they took me right up into the
mountains, from where we looked down on
the river shimmering in the intense heat. But
I could tell that they were itching to get back
and check the progress at the swim.

Hunkering down

We made our way to the river and found their client, Alan Welsh, who had booked to fish what they call a "hardcore" session. This entails fishing an entire week on the riverbank, and I had come in the middle of Alan's attempt to beat his personal best, a 46-lb (21-kg) catfish. There really is nothing to this fishing but to trust in the expertise of Dave, Karen, and Paul and settle down to put in plenty of hours, hoping that at some time or another one of the bite alarms will signal its warning.

Dave explained to me that, although the chances of catching a big catfish during the oppressive heat of the day were minimal, you still have to keep the rods out, for there is always that slim chance. Catfish tend to hunt for food at night, and their favorite morsels are snatched from the big carp population, along with a few mullet. I had always naively assumed that catfish hunted tight to the riverbed, but Dave, who has spent literally thousands of hours fishing on the Ebro riverbank, told me that I was quite wrong.

"I had come in the middle of Alan's attempt to beat his personal best..."

NO BEAUTY The catfish is perhaps not the prettiest of trophy fish, but Alan, vacationing in Spain for a week, was obviously delighted with his bewhiskered captive.

THE ENVIRONMENT

The Ebro is the largest single outflow of water in Spain and is fed by over 200 tributaries. It carves a spectacular course before discharging into the Mediterranean some 100 miles (160 km) south of Barcelona. Fishing for catfish is centered downstream at the towns of Amposta, Tortosa, and Mora, within easy reach of the coast.

Temperatures are relatively moderate at this final stretch of the river. July, August, and September are the hottest months at 70–73°F (21–22°C). January is coldest, averaging at 48°F (9°C).

Rainfall and sunshine Rainfall is greater on the eastern coast than in the dry interior of Spain. The Ebro delta thus has a relatively gentle climate. November is the wettest month.

Key fish include wels catfish, growing in excess of 200 lb (90 kg), as well as many varieties of carp, some weighing in at over 40 lb (18 kg), and barbel.

Other fish found in great quantity in the lower Ebro are black bass, mullet, zander, rudd, and roach, all of them preyed upon by the river's mighty catfish (the reason the catfish grow to such a tremendous size).

Prime time for catfishing is between February and late October, mainly because the Ebro is prone to severe flooding in winter.

SEEN BY DAYLIGHT This catfish was caught the previous night and safely roped up in the river. My guide Dave (*above*) firmly pulled it to the shore to be photographed with Alan, who had wrestled with it for more than an hour. Both of them are seen lifting its massive bulk clear of the water before its release back into the Ebro River.

"Alongside the boats I could see a huge shape snaking around in the dimly lit water..."

Dave's theory is that catfish tend to lie on the bottom in a corpulent state for most of the day, and then rise up out of the depths to feed as the sun dips and temperatures drop a little. I was left to imagine the massive predators prowling the river at night, just below the surface, and forever zeroing in on hapless carp and mullet—it sent shivers down my spine.

I had elected to stay on the riverbank for this trip, but no catfish sniffed at my bait. Dave, Karen, and Alan went out in their boats to drift live bait out among the margins, where sometimes the creatures could be heard leaping clear of the water as they ripped into unsuspecting prey. But the real story was of a monster that Alan had lost two days previously, when the giant fish had gone for one more powerful dive and had parted the mainline. Catfishing may be a waiting game, but hearing stories like that certainly pumps up the adrenaline levels and helps to keep you alert.

Struggling in the dark

The second evening, as the sun disappeared behind the distant mountains, the boat crew once again put their gear into the vessel and motored off to drift the far bank. Paul and I could do no more than sit by the rods on the bank and hope that one of the alarms would sound. Even when tiredness sets in, and you go off to sleep in your tent, you know that the alarm will wake you should a fish call.

At around midnight, the silence of the river was shattered by a loud and penetrating scream from Alan. Paul and I could hear that he had hooked a catfish, but the scene was all the more eerie for the fact that we could hear but not see what was going on. Across the water

we could hear Dave in his boat calling out advice, and also some heartfelt cursing from Alan when the fish obviously went into another dive. The struggle continued in the darkness for another half-hour, and then we saw them slowly returning with their prize. Alongside the boats I could see a huge shape snaking around in the dimly lit water. The fish was gently roped off to be photographed the next day, and already the camp was buzzing; as anglers do, we sat around and heard every detail of the fight. The catfish was estimated at around 50–60 lb (24–28 kg), so no giant, but a more than welcome sight and a proper reward for Alan's perseverance. It is hard to imagine a catfish over three times that size.

Caught napping

My third and final night on the Ebro saw me fast asleep until my dreams were shattered by the sudden, shrill sound of an alarm. In a single moment of pure, blind, sleep-interrupted panic, I crashed out of my tent, tripped over the guy rope, and fell to the ground. The fish was rushing away as I picked myself up, but— in what seemed like a one-fingered gesture from a laughing catfish—it then decided to drop the bait and recede to the depths again. The classic dropped take is not unexpected to any hunter of predatory fish; all any of us can do is hope for better the next time.

One thing, though, I have deliberately left until the end; as much as catfish have become synonymous with the Ebro, they are not actually indigenous to the river. Thirty years ago, a group of German anglers released a number of small catfish into the waters. I wonder if they know what lurks there now.

ALTERNATIVE LOCATIONS

If you want big catfish, you need to chase the wels variety; the big specimens are predominantly taken from European waters.

Russia
The Volga delta is becoming increasingly popular among roaming catfish anglers; catching a 200-lb (90-kg) monster there is an ever-present possibility. Live bait is used, with local species such as ide being used as the bait.

Kazakhstan
Fishing in this former state of the Soviet Union, some pioneering anglers are catching huge wels catfish on live bait. Their success suggests that many rivers in Europe could hold a strong head of these fish.

Danube River, Germany
While huge numbers of German anglers visit the Ebro in Spain for catfishing vacations, the species is also found in the mighty Danube. In Germany the catfish has achieved cult status, and German anglers are renowned for roving in search of better sport.

TACKLE & TECHNIQUES

Heavy-duty fishing gear is a common sight in the context of sea fishing, but nowhere have I seen such heavy rods and reels used for a freshwater species as on the banks of the Ebro. The catfish professionals know that they may be facing a battle with a fish of more than 100 lb (45 kg), and they have equipment to match. Subtlety has its place in fishing, but if the fish are always lost, subtlety has to give way to practicality.

Fishing from the bank

When fishing from the bank, Dave and Paul prefer to have four of their big rods set up at one time, which greatly increases their chance of success during a long session. The rods rest on a custom-built rod-pod; the handles are tied to the pod with bungy-cord in case a reel jams when a catfish is running.

A separate bait is attached to each of the four rods. The baits are set close to the surface because catfish feed at that level. Bulky live bait is always used for catfishing, so casting out the bait is not an option. Instead, Dave and Paul have devised a most ingenious system for anchoring free-swimming bait out in the main river flow.

A series of plastic bottles are left at anchor to float on the surface at the head of the swim. To change one of the live baits, Dave chugs out in the boat with the hooked-up live bait attached to a line; Paul stands on the bank and plays out the line from the reel. Anchoring at a bottle, Dave attaches the end rig to the bottle via a weak link of line, so that the live bait can swim freely. Should a catfish eventually take the live bait, the weak line to the bottle breaks instantly,

ROD-POD *(below)* Dave fishes four rods at a time, all attached to a sturdy pod.

HEAVY-DUTY REELS *(below)* Unsurprisingly, durability is the number-one consideration in all catfishing gear.

leaving you with just the fish at the end of the line and no bottle attached. This technique may sound complicated, but in practice it is simple and outstandingly effective; the live bait can swim, yet it remains essentially in the desired position—out in deep water and near the surface—and it cannot tangle the other lines; most important, it comes free from the bottle if taken by a catfish.

Fishing from a boat

Catfishing is simpler from a boat. The crew move to the swim and fish their live bait under simple floats, allowing the bait to swim as naturally as possible. Drifting the live bait from a boat carries them over far more ground, and the boat can even be directed toward the splashes made by catfish breaching the surface. Areas inaccessible from the riverbank can be fished easily, and a large catfish that has been hooked can be followed in a boat as it makes its powerful runs. However, it is never wise to try to bring such a fish into the boat.

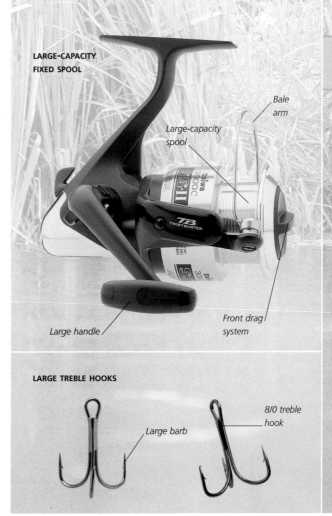

LARGE-CAPACITY FIXED SPOOL

Bale arm

Large-capacity spool

Front drag system

Large handle

LARGE TREBLE HOOKS

Large barb

8/0 treble hook

RIVER FISHING FOR CATFISH

Rods Dave McCoy was using rods specially built in Spain to his specifications. About 7 ft (2 m) long, they were powerful, equating to an 8-lb (3.5-kg) test curve.

Reels Very big Daiwa and Shimano fixed-spool reels were used, mainly because most of Dave's clients are accustomed to using fixed-spools for carp fishing.

Lines When used from the bank, reels were loaded with 45-lb (20-kg) mono. For use aboard the boats, the reels were equipped with 80-lb (36-kg) braid.

Traces These were razor-sharp trebles, all tied onto 80-lb (36-kg) Dacron. This wound kind of traceline seems best able to resist the catfish's mouth.

USING THE TAPE *(below)* Catfishers are especially eager to get the measure of their catches.

MOUTH OF A PREDATOR *(below)* All tackle, but especially the hooks, must be of top quality to prevent loss of these enormous fish.

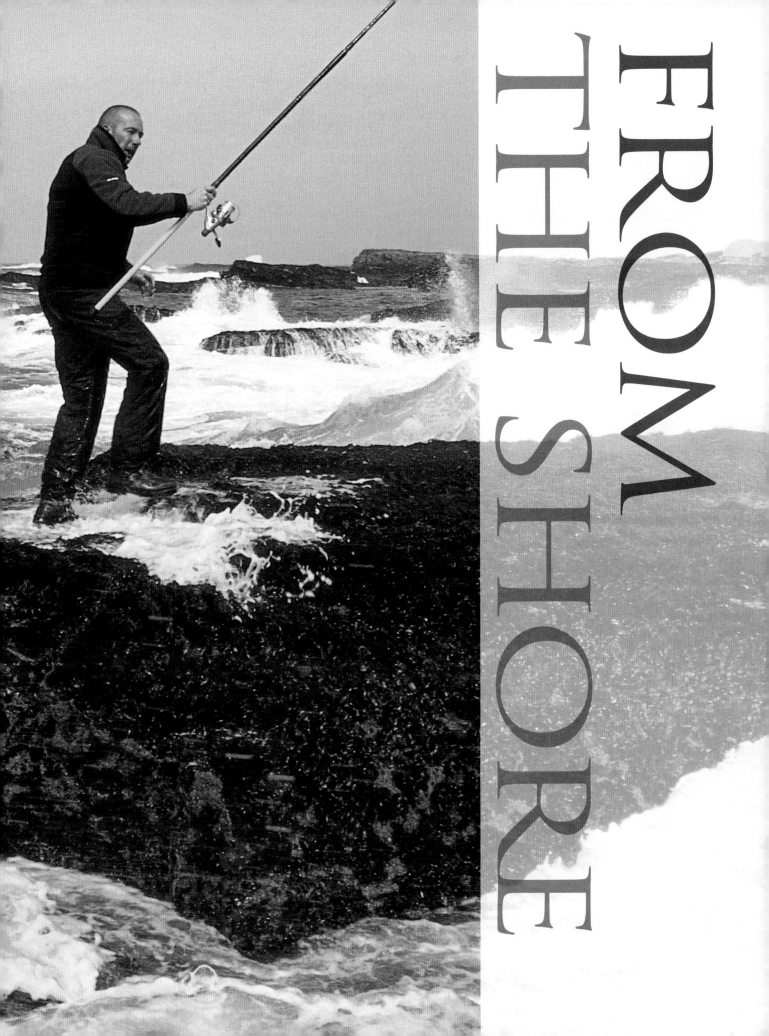

FROM
THE
SHORE

"Imagine hooking a shark that weighs more than you do, and then watching as your reel nearly empties of line..."

Compared to boat fishermen, who can follow a hooked fish as it runs and gain line doing so, shore-based anglers must literally think on their feet. Once the fish is hooked, only fast thought and sometimes a lot of brawn can bring in the fish. Shore fishing is practiced wherever fish pass close to a coast that can be accessed by an intrepid angler.

As I hope to demonstrate in the following account of my first shore-fishing trip, estuary mullet fishing is the calmer, more reflective side of shore fishing, often taking place in quiet waterways and secluded creeks. The mullet itself is unusual in being a sea fish that is often stalked and caught in ways more readily associated with game fishing, and with tackle usually selected for coarse fishing. Estuary mulleting is an extremely seductive form of fishing, yet many people continue to believe that mullet are among the most difficult fish to catch.

My second trip took me to Jersey, the biggest of the Channel Islands, which has some of the best fishing for sea bass in Europe. I discovered that local knowledge of the island's waters and fishing locations is indispensable, since the tidal range is one of the most extreme in the world. I found a unique environment and perfect light, and plenty of fish to be caught with light tackle and quick thinking.

Magical fishing in Ireland

On the next trip, the immense estuary of Ireland's Shannon River seemed a fairly daunting place to fish, but any hesitation was quickly dispelled when thornback ray and the occasional bull huss kept the rod tips rattling throughout the day. I was fishing for those species at least 25 miles (40 km) from the open sea, ample proof that, when you are fishing in Ireland, none of the usual rules seem to apply.

From the Irish coast my next trip took me to the east coast of Florida, where I fished the opposing side of the Atlantic Ocean from a variety of beaches and jetties. My companion was Roger Mortimore, the former long-distance casting champion for England, and our intention was to try our European methods in well fished areas of the state. Casting our bait into deeper water than the American anglers, we certainly enjoyed success, but even so we quickly adopted local methods and types of bait to fish from the many piers. With so many species and locations, Florida has all the fishing anyone could want.

The pollack is a true adversary, and there is nowhere better to fish for it than from the shore on the west coast of Ireland. On this trip we had to take every day's weather as it came, for here the Atlantic sets its own rules; the foolhardy angler who ventures out onto the exposed rocky ledges when the wind is up can expect trouble, and walls of crashing water frequently make the fishing temporarily impossible. Trying to prevent a pollack's crash dive to the bottom is always a mean, no-holds-barred affair, but these humble, often overlooked fish epitomize the spirit of shore fishing in its purest form.

My last shore-fishing trip, to the Skeleton Coast of Namibia, was extraordinary. The action is not subtle, but your heart races unnaturally fast when you pit yourself against the big sharks patrolling just off the desolate beaches. Imagine hooking a shark that weighs more than you do, and then watching as your reel nearly empties of line; all you can do is plant your feet in the sand and do battle with a true predator. Hooking the sharks is not the challenge; it is how much punishment your body can take, and how often can you say that about fishing? Namibia, without question, is the extreme side of shore fishing.

ESTUARY MULLET FISHING
IN SOUTHWEST ENGLAND

There can be few more glorious pastimes than wandering the rockier coastlines of southwest England, but a whole new world opens up when at the same time you are looking for shoals of feeding mullet. Many anglers chase mullet on the open coast, but perhaps the purest form of the sport takes place on lonely estuary banks and their countless hidden inlets. This is a kind of fishing where an inclination toward solitude is beneficial; on the whole, anglers in crowds leave disappointed.

The mullet is not known as the gray ghost for nothing. When you fish its haunts in the estuaries of southwest England, a few dark shadows can appear as if from nowhere and then, frustratingly, swim on up the estuary. Ignoring you and your bait, they leave no sign that they were there; a bow-wave from a fish's dorsal fin may be the only calling card you will see. Mullet anglers know the difficulty of inducing a bite from perfectly visible shoals, as well as the species' uncanny ability to shed a hook. But memories of the bite, strike, and initial run of a good mullet, plus its sheer fighting power, provide ample compensation.

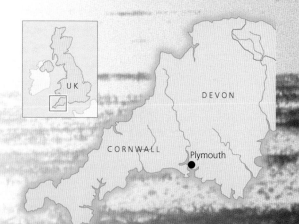

"Mullet spook easily, and the last thing you want is to scare away the shoal..."

One day in early March saw a small group of us making the journey over the Tamar Bridge from Plymouth in Devon, west and into the heart of Cornwall. The previous few days had been mild and without much rain, so we fully expected to find our favorite creek in good condition. Nobody else was around when we pulled up, unsurprising really, since at this time of year most anglers are focused on the spring run of cod, or maybe a big thornback ray, and most definitely on the coming pollack sport on the inshore reefs. But if you live in a "mild" area and have not had heavy storms all winter, you have a good chance of finding mullet.

Stalking the mullet

The tide still had maybe an hour to go before we stood any chance of seeing mullet, so we sat down and waited in the spring sunshine for the waters to rise. Good estuary mullet spots such as this one have trees that you can climb to get a good view down into the water. We scrambled up, slipped on polarizing sunglasses,

and began to scout for mullet. Sure enough, as the waters rose, a few mullet began to mill around; were they about to feed?

We had brought bread to scatter on the surface and now threw in some pieces, even though mullet tend to ignore such offerings until suddenly they instinctively turn and feed. That is when you hope they will take the piece of bread with your hook in it. It seemed unlikely that they would feed instantly, but you never know. As the tide rose higher and pushed up the creek, the chances of the mullet feeding increased, even more so when there was enough water for some of them to push on up into the pool in front of us. It was tempting to fish for them right away, but a good ambush calls for a degree of patience. Mullet spook easily, and the last thing you want is to scare away the shoal.

We followed the mullet, throwing in more bread, until finally some of the fish turned and began to feed on pieces that were lying both on the bottom and on the surface.

GRAY GHOST The mullet fisherman must take an avid interest in the local weather and tides; both exert a direct influence on the movements of mullet shoals.

THE ENVIRONMENT

Southwest England has many rivers and streams flowing from upland moors that rise to 2,000 ft (600 m). Toward Cornwall their steep-sided valleys are drowned at the coast due to tilting of the land. The river estuaries are rich sources of fish, and some species travel inland in the safety of the deep-water inlets.

Temperatures in the region are warmer than in most areas of the UK due to its far southwestern position and the moderating effect of the Gulf Stream. In Plymouth the coolest months are January and February, averaging 43°F (6°C); July and August are warmest, at 61°F (16°C).

Rainfall and sunshine The Southwest bears the brunt of rainfall from the Atlantic, making it one of the wettest parts of the country. The annual average is 40 in (1,014 mm), which compares to 35 in (897 mm) for England and Wales.

Key fish in the estuaries include mullet (golden gray, thick-lipped, and thin-lipped), bass, and flounder.

Other fish can include mackerel, garfish, wrasse, pollack, bull huss, black bream, coalfish, conger eel, and rays.

Prime time for mullet in southwest England is between February and November. In the winter months you need a respite from stormy weather for any real chance of success.

ALTERNATIVE LOCATIONS

Falkland Islands
There are big, ocean-going mullet in the Southern Atlantic that enjoy feeding on fresh lamb bait.

Gibraltar
Vast shoals of mullet are to be found all over the Mediterranean, but mullet specialists have noted that the biggest fish seem to be found around various marinas in Gibraltar.

Alderney, Channel Islands
Anyone interested in mullet fishing has either fished or dreams of fishing the tiny island of Alderney. Lying some 8 miles (13 km) off the French coast, it is visited by big shoals of open-coast mullet that winter off the rocky coastline. I have seen huge mullet in the area, and many people anticipate that the mullet record for the British Isles—over 14 lb (6 kg)—will one day be held by an Alderney fish.

"Within a split second the rod tip slammed over and battle commenced..."

We had mullet in front of us and they were feeding. This was a golden opportunity to fish for them; tomorrow might bring gales and rain, and then we would be back to cod fishing.

Some of our group wandered off to the other bank to try for the odd big fish that might be moving up a deeper gully. I stayed put and gently cast some weighted bait to the head of the pool, which any fish would pass on its way in. Right away there were little taps on the rod tip, but I could see that fish were only nudging at the bread and flicking the mainline with their tails.

All anglers know how hard it is to refrain from striking when the rod tip bounces. Unable to look two ways at once, you must drag your eyes away from the fish and back to the rod tip, and wait for that moment to strike. You have to control your natural reflex to sweep back the rod, have patience, and give the fish time to start feeding with confidence. In a perfect world, of course, the mullet would hit the bread bait so hard that the fine tip would slam over, and every time you would strike with perfect timing and hook the fish.

A strike too soon

In the end, I spectacularly missed the first bite and was rewarded by having my little lead sinker whistle right past my nose and on into the trees behind. And it would happen just as the mullet were beginning to really feed (not a common sight in my experience). I had struck so hard that my end tackle was now tangled up in the trees behind me. Do you ever feel like taking your rod and simply snapping it over your knee in sheer frustration?

But, with a little bit of calm thinking and an extremely swift untanglement, I was soon back to fishing. The very next cast and a fish was on, albeit not a monster. A spirited fight ensued, but already I wanted to take a shot at some larger mullet that were now coming in. With all haste I released my mullet and cast out once more to where the bigger fish lay, thinking that by now they must be spooked. Wrong. Within a split second, the rod tip slammed over and battle commenced, with my quarry charging straight across the pool and scattering all the fish in its path. The reel's clutch shrieked its protest against the streaming line, but then came the point when a fish can run no farther. What happens in that split second is mostly down to luck, for mullet like to head for the nearest snag, where your line

breaks up. But just occasionally the fish makes a mistake and heads back for clear water, and then, if the hook does not come out, you know that the fish is going to be yours.

Gray mullet: Britain's bonefish?

Early-season mullet fight as though they have wintered in a gym, so if you are lucky enough to hook one, hang on and enjoy the power. As the net slips underneath your mullet, witness one of Britain's ultimate fish. Mine was around the 5-lb (2.25-kg) mark and a good specimen.

Mullet are not fish the size of submarines, as some species can seem to be, yet that matters little to those anglers who pursue the gray ghosts. There is no worthier challenge in our estuarine waters; there are vast tracts of water waiting to be fished, and nowhere do you have to pay for the privilege. If you get to know the mullet, you will understand why some anglers proudly call it the British bonefish.

SURVEYING THE ESTUARY
Incoming mullet often can be seen directly from the shoreline. A better vantage point can be gained by climbing a tree, although for safety's sake this should never be attempted alone. Scattering bread on the water helps to keep feeding fish interested. My friend, Chris Woollven, is holding a splendid specimen that he enticed from the estuary's tangled seaweed.

TACKLE & TECHNIQUES

Rod and reel technologies do not offer any great advantage in mulleting. Your greatest asset is an open mind and the ability to "read" a situation while it unfolds before you. Mullet fishing is not for the angler who prefers to stay in one place all day. You need to walk along the shore, look around, and experiment. Polarizing sunglasses and a pair of waders are indispensable.

Mullet fishing is attractive because there are so many ways to catch them from so many places. Few of my home species offer this variety. When fishing for conger eel, for example, it is necessary to put fresh bait hard on the seabed in the general area where the conger are believed to be; ledgering (in which the bait is weighted before being cast out) is the method used. Ledgering may be suitable for mullet also, if the fish are mostly invisible and if they are feeding in a particular way. But in different conditions it may be more appropriate to try freelining, surface fishing, or float fishing. There really is no right or wrong way to fish for mullet, and I am always ready to adopt new methods and adapt existing ones if I find that they work. The challenge is to be flexible enough to change your methods as necessary, all the time you are out.

Fishing is the art of outwitting fish, and lifting a mullet from among a shoal that you can see in the water can be very difficult. Nobody could ever accuse the wary mullet of being an easy quarry, but that is the attraction of the species.

SIGHT FISHING *(below left)* Spotting incoming fish is one of the thrills of mullet fishing.

MULLET MARKS *(below)* These "scrapes" are caused by the mouths of feeding mullet.

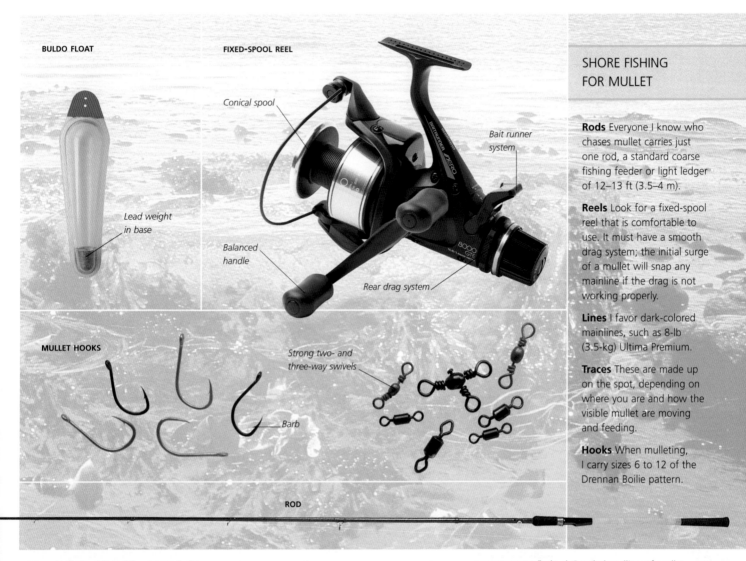

BULDO FLOAT

Lead weight in base

FIXED-SPOOL REEL

Conical spool

Bait runner system

Balanced handle

Rear drag system

MULLET HOOKS

Barb

Strong two- and three-way swivels

ROD

SHORE FISHING FOR MULLET

Rods Everyone I know who chases mullet carries just one rod, a standard coarse fishing feeder or light ledger of 12–13 ft (3.5–4 m).

Reels Look for a fixed-spool reel that is comfortable to use. It must have a smooth drag system; the initial surge of a mullet will snap any mainline if the drag is not working properly.

Lines I favor dark-colored mainlines, such as 8-lb (3.5-kg) Ultima Premium.

Traces These are made up on the spot, depending on where you are and how the visible mullet are moving and feeding.

Hooks When mulleting, I carry sizes 6 to 12 of the Drennan Boilie pattern.

BREAD BAIT (*below*) Bread for use as bait is an essential part of the mullet angler's gear.

A LIGHT TOUCH (*below*) Gentle handling of mullet is essential to their safe return to the water.

LURE FISHING FOR SEA BASS IN THE CHANNEL ISLANDS

The Channel Islands offer the roving angler all possible terrains: classic beaches where the rhythmic pattern of the surf soothes the soul; huge, man-made breakwaters and piers; and every kind of rock mark you can imagine. Deep water turning from deep blue to inky black, shallow water in all shades of turquoise, rough water, tidal water—the islands have them all. Anglers accustomed to overcrowded fishing are among the first to appreciate that recreational angling is not a large-scale local pursuit in the Channel Islands; and you can fish virtually anywhere without charge.

Jersey, and indeed all of the Channel Islands, could be considered a mecca for bass angling. The sea bass is a true sporting quarry and is targeted by all kinds of anglers, whether they be fishing bait, lure, or fly. Bass are predatory fish that rely on speed, agility, and subtlety to ensnare their prey. And everywhere you look in the Channel Islands seems to suggest bass; every inlet, beach, gully, reef, rock, tidal rip, weed raft, and harbor looks perfect for the predators that anglers like to call "the wolves of the sea."

JERSEY

Rozel

JERSEY

St. Ouen's Bay

St. Aubin

Corbière

St. Helier

La Roque Pt.

"For successful lure fishing you need to find areas where bass like to lurk..."

The Channel Islands are famous for the incredible rise and fall of their tides, and what the receding waters expose twice a day is awe-inspiring. Go at high water to the southeast corner of Jersey, toward the area flanking the imposing Seymour Tower off La Roque Point, and you will notice a few rocks poking their heads from the surface. Return a few hours later and you will see what resembles a lunar landscape that had been there all along, ready to rip the hull from any unsuspecting boat. Tracts of aggressive-looking rocky formations; great rafts of weed; crisp, virgin sand; and innumerable shallow gullies all show themselves. Jersey doubles in size twice a day, and to any angler this tidal movement and array of features can mean only one thing: fish.

Seeking out the quarry

Lure fishing for bass is growing steadily in popularity on the islands, with more and more anglers using lighter tackle and high-tech lures of plastic and metal. You don't put bait out there and then play the waiting game for a bite, as indeed I do most of the time. Instead, you find the fish by staying mobile and casting lures into as many different areas as possible. It can be a very visual form of fishing, especially when using surface lures. The bass has to rise up and try to snatch the imitation fish right off the top of the water as you retrieve it back toward you. Sometimes the fish will swirl two or three times around the lure and then finally smash into it with the ferocity of a tiger. For successful lure fishing, you need to find areas where bass like to lurk and snaffle prey; it just so happens that almost all of the Jersey coastline is perfect for this kind of fishing.

A surface-lure specialist

My guide and companion for the week on Jersey was a bass fanatic by the name of Andrew Syvret. It seems that we had almost crossed paths at Plymouth University, but while I was searching out treacherous cliff marks on stormy winter nights, Andrew had been looking for bass locations; as a result, we had never even met. Now he is happy to spend all of his fishing time back home pursuing bass on surface-fished lures.

LURE LORE The inventiveness of the lure manufacturers is fully tested in the Channel Islands; if the bass don't perceive the lures as baitfish, they won't attack them.

THE ENVIRONMENT

Jersey is the largest of the Channel Islands and lies 90 miles (145 km) south of the English coast. Its 50-mile (80-km) coast harbors many fish species. The shoreline ranges from flat, sandy beaches to high, rocky cliffs. Jersey has one of the largest tidal movements in the world—tides can differ by as much as 40 ft (12 m) from low and high water.

Temperatures are warmer than any other part of the British Isles, averaging 63°F (17°C) in summer. Winter temperatures are mild, averaging 43°F (6°C).

Rainfall and sunshine Average rainfall is 34 in (860 mm), yet Jersey has the most sun in the British Isles, with an average of 1,915 hours of sunshine.

Key fish include bass, pollack, wrasse, and mullet.

Other fish in Jersey waters include flatfish, rays, bream, dogfish, mackerel, garfish, pouting, conger eel, and John Dory. Sunfish and basking sharks may be seen in summer.

Prime time for lure fishing for bass begins around the end of March and lasts into November. Bass can be found year-round in the Channel Islands, but lure fishing is prevented by very rough winter conditions. Consequently, the bait angler takes over in that season.

SEARCHING FOR BASS Wading onto shallow sandbanks to roam around with minimal tackle is a way of fishing much more common in the Florida Keys—where it is used for tarpon and sharks—than in the British Isles. Clear water is essential for sight-fishing; you must be able to see the progress of your lure on the surface. In Channel Island waters it is preferable to wear chest waders for insulation against the cold.

"We pulled on chest waders and our essential polarizing sunglasses..."

You would think that a popular vacation destination such as Jersey would have people wandering every bit of coastline, but most of the tourists seem unwilling to leave the sanctuary of a busy beach. Therefore we were left alone and uncrowded, able to roam wherever Andrew felt bass might lurk, waiting for the tide to come in or recede to the point when the unknown stimulant in a bass's brain makes it suddenly go on the feed.

Into the ebbing tide

Following Andrew through unknown, criss-crossed back lanes, my thoughts were on what lay ahead, for it was impossible to build a mental map of where we were going. We soon turned into a small clearing, where we pulled on chest waders and our essential polarizing sunglasses before diving down through an invisible gap in the hedge.

Reaching the gully Andrew had targeted, we had to wade into the waters just as they began to ebb. I am about 6 ft (1.8 m) tall, but Andrew is a little bit taller, so he could begin wading perhaps 10 minutes before me. I was aware that I had all my angling photographer's gear on my back, and I did not relish the prospect of applying to my insurance company yet again for damaged equipment. While I waited, one part of my brain wished Andrew every early success, for after all this was his patch, but another part could not help but hope that maybe he would take a dunking; of course, I never would have laughed. But he succeeded in throwing some lures at what he promised was the best stage of the tide.

ALTERNATIVE LOCATIONS

Montauk, New York
There are many areas where the famous striped bass are caught, but Montauk, on the extreme eastern tip of Long Island, New York, has always captured my imagination. European and American bass can be caught using very similar lure-fishing techniques.

Ebro River, Spain
Some very large sea bass run a long distance up the Ebro, and they are very catchable on lures. The best time to try is in the early evening.

Northwest France
Lure fishing for sea bass is hugely popular on the northern Atlantic coast of France, which has many of the reefy, shallow grounds that the fish prefer.

"For two perfect hours we threw our lures wherever we could physically cast them..."

As I sat there, my eyes caught Andrew's rod whipping back into the unmistakable curve of a take, and heard his excited voice carrying across the water. He was into a bass and it was without doubt a good fish. Wanting to record his catch for posterity, I called out: "Andrew, whatever you do, get this fish in!" My friend knew full well what he was doing, as he was about to demonstrate. Sure enough, after several of the heart-stopping moments typical of a real predator's fight, the glint of silver-barred bass was in his hands, and then there was that unmistakable, beaming smile that breaks over the face of a successful angler. Sometimes it helps to be a little taller.

The size of catches to come?

Anglers know that fishing does not often work out like this, especially on the first afternoon of a trip away, but just occasionally things go perfectly and you become certain that you have a magical few days in store. When, within 10 minutes of the first session, your companion catches over 10 lb (4.5 kg) of perfect, glinting, lure-caught bass, what more could you ask for? Many people will go a lifetime without ever seeing, never mind landing, a shore-caught bass of that size. It was a perfect start to the trip but, as luck would have it, we did not see that size of fish again while I was there.

Did that seem some sort of anticlimax? In fact, it did not at all. We caught plenty more "normal" bass, and to see wild bass surging and smashing into surface lures like wolves into a carcass left me with some unforgettable images. Just to fish among like-minded people and on deserted coastlines is a privilege that can never diminish, wherever I am lucky enough to be.

But, perhaps oddly, my greatest memories of those few days came from a fishless session. Sometimes the conditions and light conspire to paint a scene that just does not need the "interruption" of a fish to make it perfect.

A sublime morning

We were on the southwest coast of Jersey at 5 am in early summer, and the rising sun was creeping up and over the length of a deserted St. Ouen's Bay. It was high tide over the causeway to Corbière lighthouse and the water was bubbling and churning through the narrow gap; it seemed like a rampant, charging animal, almost snarling with ferocity. This description may seem an exaggeration, but you need to see the tides in Jersey to appreciate just how aggressive the water can look, even with no storm behind it to whip it up.

As the sun caught the stark white of the lighthouse, we remained in slight shadow and the sea crashed and surged around us. For two perfect hours we threw our lures wherever we could physically cast them, and yet not a sign of a fish. Bass usually love a lot of movement in the water, and the conditions could not have appeared more fruitful, but we did not catch a single thing. Moments like this are a reminder that nature always has an ace up its sleeve; securing a trophy is never a certainty.

As we set off to find some breakfast and coffee, we talked about where the next session was going to be and when the bass might feed. We had just fished two short hours in light and conditions so sublime that the lack of fish was not even an issue; you can just bet, though, that a return trip there on a lifeless day would throw up a monster fish.

CASTING FOR BASS Jersey's coastline has numerous inlets where casting lures is possible from the waterside. The bigger fish tend to cluster around rocks, so wading the rocky gullies toward them can bring success. The bass was the first caught by Andrew, my guide on the trip; at over 10 lb (4.5 kg), it was an exceptional size for a shore-caught fish.

TACKLE & TECHNIQUES

Casting lures for bass, as for any species, depends primarily on good information on the whereabouts of the fish. You need to know that fish are in the vicinity, how far out they are, and the depths at which they are swimming. Your main concern then is how to present your lure and retrieve it in the most natural-looking and attractive way possible.

Some anglers prefer the stretch and "loose" feel of mono lines when casting lures, although others are coming to prefer high-quality braided lines. Working relatively lightweight lures in specific ways through or on top of the water benefits from the direct, no-stretch feel of braid, and braid is far more responsive and perhaps a little more exciting when a fish is hooked.

Newcomers to lure fishing are easily bewildered by the huge range of lures on offer. When fishing for bass, it is best to keep your tackle as uncluttered as possible. See what other anglers are using and buy a few of those lures; then carry with you only the lures that have proved their worth in the past.

Depending on how the fish are behaving, you will need lures designed to dive deep, hang in the midwater, travel just below the surface, or even flail along on top of the surface. Surface fishing is perhaps the most exciting form, although you have to overcome initial skepticism that a big predator will attack a piece of rubber or plastic being fished on top of the water. But when that happens, you will understand the thrill.

TOOLS OF THE TRADE *(below left)* How you work a lure is as important in fishing as the lure itself.

WINNING LOOK *(below)* Worked on the surface like a distressed fish, this lure can be irresistible.

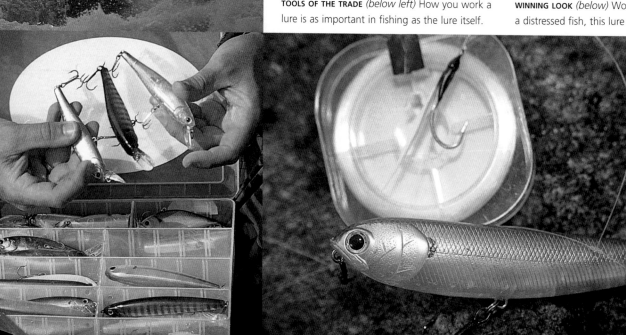

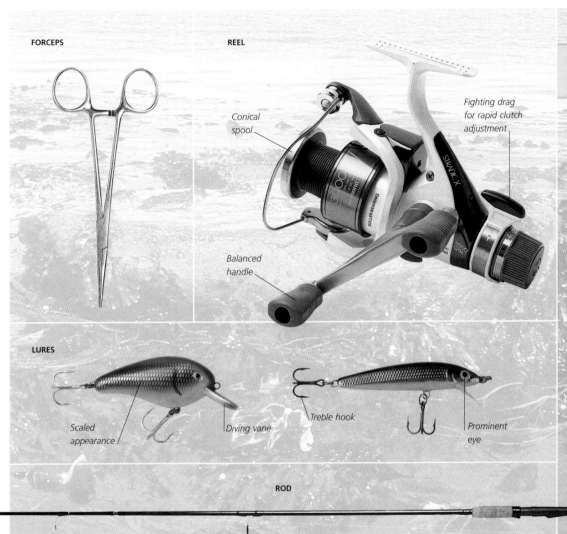

FORCEPS

REEL

Conical
spool

*Fighting drag
for rapid clutch
adjustment*

Balanced
handle

LURES

Scaled
appearance

Diving vane

Treble hook

Prominent
eye

ROD

LURE FISHING FOR BASS

Rods Whereas a 12-ft (3.6-m) carp rod can be used for lure fishing, anglers are turning increasingly to 9–10-ft (2.5–3-m) lure rods. These are extremely light and are able to cast light lures a long way.

Reels A good-quality fixed-spool reel from either Shimano or Daiwa can be used, or a small multiplier of the baitcasting type.

Lines Mono line in the 10–15-lb (4.5–6.5-kg) range is perfect. You may like to tie on a 30-lb (13.5-kg) shockleader. Braid is also a possibility; try both and see which one you prefer.

Hooks Most lures have integrated treble hooks; more than three trebles can make unhooking difficult.

DEEP WATER *(below)* Jersey's rock marks can give access to strong tidal rips, beloved by bass.

JOINTED LURE *(below)* This bass may have been attracted by the lure's lifelike swimming motion.

SURGICAL PRECISION *(below)* Using forceps for unhooking can cause less suffering to the fish.

SHORE FISHING FOR IRISH THORNBACK RAY

Anglers have long fished their shorelines for ray species, including the small-eyed, spotted, blonde, undulate, and the thornback. But why fish for such weird-looking creatures? Perhaps it is our sense that they belong to another, prehistoric time period; the sight of a ray "kiting" toward you as you reel it in is unique in angling. Rays may also be targeted in many ways, and at all times of the year; use different baits, different tactics, and you still catch them. Commercial pressure is reducing the numbers of small-eyed and spotted rays, so now there is greater interest in the thornback, along with the bull huss, which looks like a giant dogfish and often inhabits similar terrain.

Thornbacks are taken from many places in Britain, but we were heading perhaps 30 miles (50 km) up the vast Shannon estuary on the west coast of Ireland. We had heard that in this relatively simple terrain we would be able to catch thornies and huss using nothing more than mackerel as bait. With rock fishing for pollack also within easy reach on the Atlantic coast, it was too good an opportunity to miss.

"We could stand close to the water and cast, and then bring back the rods..."

THORNY DEFENSES The thornback ray is protected by remarkably effective camouflage as well as the rows of thorns that give it its name.

The six of us had traveled to Ireland with a two-part plan; after sampling the pollack fishing on the coast at Kilkee, we would try to catch thornback ray and bull huss on the Shannon River. But the local rock marks were under bombardment by vast Atlantic swells, so we turned our attention to the inland estuary waters. This was a new place for all of us and in some respects we were reliant on information supplied by previous visitors. Surely they were wrong in advising us to head 30 miles (50 km) upstream before starting?

Simple mackerel bait

Around our local section of coastline we would normally take a variety of bait for these two species, including peeler crabs, live shrimp, squid, sand eels, and ragworm. But we had been told in no uncertain terms that the only offering we needed to present was mackerel, either caught off the rocks, bought locally, or used in the blast-frozen Ammo form. Duly purchasing mackerel, therefore, we packed our tackle and bait into our minibus, turned east from Kilkee, and drove toward a mark called Labasheeda, situated on the north bank of the Shannon.

Parking at the side of the road, we walked just a short distance down to a classic estuary mark: comfortable rocky platforms for casting and fishing, a weed-strewn foreshore, and then murky water. Doubting that we would find fish at our first attempt on this vast expanse of water, we rapidly put beachcasters together, strapped on small multipliers, cut the mackerel into sections, and baited our traces with various cuts of mackerel flesh. It was dead low water, so we could stand close to the edge and cast, and then bring back the rods to lie in the tripods. I also set up my camera gear, and then settled down to see what would happen in the bright and breezy conditions.

THE ENVIRONMENT

The Shannon is Ireland's longest river, flowing 240 miles (386 km) from the north of the island to its vast estuary in the southwest. The Irish Tourist Board has produced a wealth of good information about fishing marks and species in every part of the river system.

Temperatures in the Shannon estuary are mild in winter, thanks to the warming influence of the Gulf Stream. January and February are the coolest months at about 41°F (5°C) on average; the warmest months are July and August, averaging 59°F (15°C).

Rainfall and sunshine Be prepared for anything and everything to come from the skies in just one day—showers are never far away. Rain is heaviest in December and January, and lightest in July. The sunniest months are May and June.

Key fish in the Labasheeda area of the lower Shannon estuary are thornback ray and bull huss.

Other fish to be found in the Shannon estuary are salmon, tope, conger eel, dogfish, bass, and flatfish.

Prime time for Irish thornbacks is from around May to October, along with the resident bull huss. In some areas both can be targeted all year, but the Shannon fishes best during the warmer months.

"You must try to lift the ray from the muddy bottom and get it heading toward you..."

When you are waiting for the first bite on a totally new mark, a short time can seem like infinity. Little demons in your head try to convince you that you are wasting your time and that nothing is going to happen—but today those voices were wrong. After what seemed like 15 very long minutes, we started to get classic ray bites. One by one, the rods were being pulled over and line was starting to peel off the reels, accompanied by the click–click sound of the ratchets.

Thornies in abundance
When you have a bite, you must give the fish time to take the bait and then set the hook; simultaneously you must try to lift the ray from the muddy bottom and get it heading toward you. The powerful "nodding" of thornback ray on the line is in a class of its own, but concerted pressure on our rods saw most of the fish come to be weighed on the scales. At first we weighed every fish before gently releasing it, but they became so numerous that after a while we stopped counting. All the fish we caught were returned to the water.

We caught all sizes, from ones no bigger than a dinner plate to a few over the magical 10-lb (4.5-kg) mark. I have fished at places around Britain that can produce really heavyweight ray of 16 lb (7.5 kg) or more, but the Shannon estuary is the only place I can think of where the seabed seems quite literally to be carpeted with fish, and all of them catchable on humble mackerel bait. Thornbacks can be caught day or night on my local coast, but only extremely rarely on simple mackerel bait. In Ireland we found that our usual squid bait did work, but really you need nothing more than fresh mackerel, or some of the good-quality frozen type.

Arrival of the bull huss
As we caught more and more ray, our hopes of also catching huss seemed increasingly remote. Huss tend to be rock-dwelling creatures and it seemed highly unlikely that they would be among the thornies. But perhaps three hours into the session and, sure enough, the huss started to feed, forcing us to make a rapid reappraisal. To Shannon anglers it may seem perfectly normal to catch bull huss at such marks, but if I were to claim the capture of a huss from my local river, people would assume I had gone crazy.

Subsequently we fished this and other marks all over the Shannon and caught good numbers of both ray and huss everywhere, although surprisingly, the daytime fishing was much better than our few night sessions. On my local coastline all huss fishing is done at night, but here they seemed more than willing to feed during the day.

Looking back, it was a great experience to return to such a straightforward form of fishing. It made me wish that fishing for all species were that simple. But times have changed and anglers have to adapt. Today, if you use any bait that works, and fish in a proactive way, the rewards can be great.

QUEST FOR RAYS With our simple mackerel bait, little time was lost in setting up before we were fishing from the rocky shoreline. Soon rays seemed to be flocking to our hooks. My friend, Rob Wheaton, is seen carefully unhooking one of his catches and then displaying it to the camera. All our rays were allowed to slide back into the Shannon.

ALTERNATIVE LOCATIONS

South Africa

This fascinating country is known for fantastic ray fishing. Ray of quite vast proportions, some of them topping 400 lb (180 kg), are caught from the beaches, especially near Cape Town. Although South African tackle is heavier than the European version, simple ledgering tactics are still used.

Queensland, Australia

Stingrays approaching 500 lb (225 kg) have been caught from Queensland piers and beaches. The monsters are landed using boat-fishing gear in the 50–80-lb (25–35-kg) class. However, the less immense stingrays encountered elsewhere in the world are caught quite easily with conventional shore tackle.

England

Many river estuaries hold populations of thornback rays, especially in Devon and Cornwall. The mouths of the Dart, Tamar, Yealm, and Fal rivers are all worth a try, as well as the large Kingsbridge estuary. The extensive Bristol Channel is famous for both cod and thornie sport.

TACKLE & TECHNIQUES

On the Shannon we found ray and huss feeding about 40–150 yd (35–135 m) out from the bank, depending on the day and state of the tide, although the flood tide tended to fish better for both species. On this river you are fishing against strong tides, not to mention great rafts of floating weed, and hooked fish try to hug the bottom all the way to the net. Ray are more attracted by static than moving bait, so the overall goal is to get the bait to the riverbed and "anchor" it there. In the fast-flowing Shannon, relatively heavy lead weights are needed to drag down the bait and keep it stationary.

We found that mackerel bait in all shapes and sizes worked well, although the tougher sections cut from the belly stayed on the hook a little better. It also paid dividends to bind the bait onto the hook with thin, elasticated thread. We used 5–6-oz (140–170-g) grip leads, mostly on the end of our typical pulley rigs, but in this river any way of nailing the bait to the bottom produces fish.

Once you have set up your baited trace, you simply cast out, let it hit the bottom, and then rest the rod in your tripod. A sturdy, 6-ft (1.8-m) tripod is essential here, since you don't want to be holding your rod all day long, and you need to keep your mainline up as high as possible. On the Shannon it is important to set the ratchet on your reel so that a biting fish can take line. This is partly because some anglers have hooked tope at least 30 miles (50 km) up the estuary; should one of those formidable fish take your bait and your ratchet is not set correctly, that may be the last you will see of your rod.

MULTIPLIER (below left) The Daiwa SLOSH 30 is highly popular as a shore-fishing reel.

BAIT Mackerel (below left) and squid (below) were used for catching thornies and bull huss.

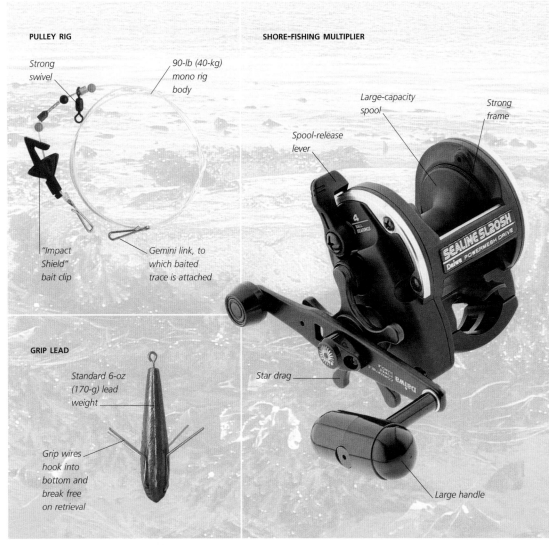

PULLEY RIG

Strong swivel

90-lb (40-kg) mono rig body

"Impact Shield" bait clip

Gemini link, to which baited trace is attached

GRIP LEAD

Standard 6-oz (170-g) lead weight

Grip wires hook into bottom and break free on retrieval

SHORE-FISHING MULTIPLIER

Spool-release lever

Large-capacity spool

Strong frame

Star drag

Large handle

SHORE FISHING FOR THORNBACK RAY

Rods A beachcaster rod of 12–13 ft (3.5–4 m) is essential for this kind of fishing. Brute lifting power is not essential, so personal preference can dictate how powerful it should be.

Reels My favorite shore-fishing reels are the Daiwa SLOSH series. They cast and fish incredibly well and most anglers I know use them.

Lines I go for a line that is tough but cheap enough to change often. Ultima Red Ice or Rough Diamond lines are very good, but if you feel like spending more, try the Ultima Tournament.

Hooks The Mustad 79515 Viking in sizes 3/0–4/0 is perfect for thornie fishing; use a trace of 80 lb (36 kg) if there are huss around.

EASY STANDING *(below)* The flat, rocky ledges by the Shannon make perfect fishing platforms.

BULL HUSS *(below right)* Fish of 10 lb (4.5 kg) or more are common, making them an attractive target.

BEACH FISHING ON FLORIDA'S EASTERN SHORE

For its size, Florida enjoys some of the world's most varied fishing. Most anglers know of the shark and tarpon fishing in the Keys, and the bass fishing in the freshwater lakes, but that is not the end of the story. Up the east coast, from the Keys to the state line, there is a world of fishing from the various beaches, inlets, and piers. Surf fishing in Florida is a huge pastime, attracting all kinds of anglers, male and female, and at every skill level. It is fantastic to see so many buzzing tackle shops, such organized fishing locations, a well run licensing and fish release/retention system, and such wholehearted respect from the fishing public for a system that works.

I quickly found out that the Florida shore anglers are completely snook crazy. A beautiful, streamlined fish, it is highly prized for both its fighting and eating qualities. Few American anglers seemed interested in the hard-fighting jacks, or indeed the vast stingrays swimming off some of the piers. European anglers, I am sure, would happily fish for those species all day.

St. Augustine

Orlando

Sebastian

FLORIDA

US

Miami

"It was obviously hugging the bottom and tracking up and down the beach..."

My plan was to meet long-distance casting champion Roger Mortimore at Orlando airport, bypass all the Florida theme parks, and head north to St. Augustine. Here Roger had a couple of contacts who thought the fishing was worth a try. This was going to be a fishing trip where we simply fished places that looked promising and continued to roam around on a quest for fish: no guides, no agenda, just common sense and, importantly, Roger's previous experience of fishing in Florida. I was in good hands.

St. Augustine

First cast, first light on a deserted beach, and my rod tip slammed over and something started ripping line off my reel. Still bleary-eyed and holding my cup of coffee, I ran to the rod and set the hook into what turned out to be a small shark. Roger had already advised me to use a wire hooklength all the time, as some of the local fish have arrays of teeth quite able to shred simple mono traces.

As the sun slowly appeared over the horizon, we settled into our fold-up chairs and kept rebaiting our traces with local mullet that we had netted the night before. Roger and I were just discussing what we should do over the next few days when his beachcaster suddenly arched over and was very nearly ripped from the stand. He jumped up and struck into a heavy fish; we had cast our bait far beyond the line of breakers, so the fish had a long way to come in. Whatever it was, Roger kept up sustained pressure from the rod and managed to turn it; we decided that it had to be a ray, for it was obviously hugging the bottom and tracking up and down the beach.

EARLY RAY My guide, Roger, displays the stingray that he caught before breakfast on the beach near St. Augustine. We estimated it to be around 30 lb (14 kg).

THE ENVIRONMENT

The Atlantic coast of Florida offers excellent beach fishing, either from the shoreline or from a number of well-known piers. We visited the beach at the northern port of St. Augustine, and the two fishing jetties at Sebastian Inlet State Recreation Area, to the south of Orlando. Inland of Sebastian, there is good fishing for freshwater species in the extensive Indian River lagoon.

Temperatures on the coast average 82°F (28°C) in summer; hot and humid weather is the norm. In winter the temperatures are kept mild by waters from the Gulf of Mexico and average around 60°F (16°C).

Rainfall and sunshine The east coast as a whole receives on average about 53 in (1,350 mm) of rainfall per year; a hurricane can bring up to 25 in (640 mm).

Key fish include snook, jacks, kingfish, and sharks.

Other fish include sheepshead, black drum, tarpon, redfish, trout, sailfish, and snapper grouper.

Prime time for snook fishing is from the beginning of September, during the snook migration.

Another 10 minutes of sustained pressure and, sure enough, the whip tail of a stingray could be seen in the shallows, thrashing around in an unmistakably menacing way. But Roger has caught plenty of these fish and knows how to handle them. He happily grabbed the stingray, held it for the camera, and then slipped it back into the warm water; it was over the 30-lb (14-kg) mark, but does that really matter? It was simply a fantastic fish, and gave us very enjoyable sport before our breakfast.

Sebastian Inlet

Later, we drove down the coast and checked into another motel on the edge of Sebastian Inlet. This is a well-known local fishing spot where we were hoping to track down some snook. Having heard so much about this fish from both Roger and some of the locals we had met in St. Augustine, I just had to see one.

At Sebastian is a narrow channel, flanked by a pier, where the sea rushes in and out of the huge Indian River that flows behind the local beaches. The tide race in the channel can be monumental, but apparently that makes perfect conditions for both snook and jacks. Either fish would do for me, but, as is usual in Florida, our first stop was to net some bait. Sure, you can walk into one of the many local tackle shops and buy what you need, but Roger wanted to show me how the locals go about throw–netting their own live bait.

SNOOK SUCCESS Roger keeps an eye on the float indicating the position of his live bait as it crashes around in the foaming waters of Sebastian Inlet. The snook is readily identified by its prominent black lateral stripe.

Apart from the fine fishing, incredible weather, and the friendliness of the angling community, the factor that amazed me most in Florida was the ease with which you can go and collect your own bait—it seems that everybody does it. Owning a throw-net is as common as owning a fishing rod, and Florida anglers are lucky in having a wealth of smaller fish that they are allowed to "harvest" as bait. Among the species caught is the mullet, which has the great misfortune to be used as bait almost everywhere. While I fish for large mullet at home purely for the sport, the fish are seen as a prime bait elsewhere, albeit in smaller sizes.

Trying for snook

At first light the next morning, we bought our permit to fish from Sebastian Pier and headed down there. Buffeted by an ever increasing onshore breeze, a few dedicated locals were already positioned in their hot spots, live-bait buckets at hand, rods all rigged up, waiting for the real push of the incoming tide. Suddenly, as if at a flick of a switch, they all hooked up with live shrimp, small majarra, or sand perch, and began to float fish just around the edge of the rocks. Roger and I would have been stupid not to have done exactly the same.

No snook came to my own bait, but I saw a few hooked and fought in the pounding seas and high winds, and that certainly seemed to explain why they are so popular. Moving upstream in small shoals, the snook were only feeding for very short periods of time. But in among the black-striped snook were the jacks. It would be an understatement to say that fishing for these jacks compensated for my lack of snook action in this part of Florida.

COMBINED EFFORT Fishing alone from the shore, reeling in line must be combined with operating the net. The operation is made a lot easier if you have a net-man to help you. A local man displays his very fine snook.

OFF THE PIER Sebastian Pier gives direct access to the fast-running channel between the Indian River and the Atlantic Ocean. Local pelicans, always looking for an easy meal, are not averse to taking anglers' live bait. I was very impressed with the sheer energy, speed, and determination of the Florida jacks, not to mention their glittering, streamlined appearance.

"I could see how well the jacks had adapted for their existence of slash, kill, and run..."

The fishing at the pier had gone quiet, so I had dispensed with the float and was simply casting out a short, flowing trace with a grip lead to hold it in place. More importantly, I had a small live majarra mounted on a very strong 4/0 hook. Resting the rod on the pier railings, I set the ratchet on the reel so that a running fish could take line instead of the rod.

Nothing happened for the first 10 minutes, so I turned to photographing the surf as it pounded in under the harsh blue sky. Just as I pressed the shutter, my reel began to scream. Sheer panic as I stuffed the camera back in the bag, picked up the rod, looked for the angle of the line, and set the hook. It was very quickly apparent that this fish was not very big, but its power, sheer speed, and ability to change direction were astonishing. Does warm water promote harder-fighting fish? Compared to equivalent coldwater fish, the local species seemed to be producing a fight out of all proportion to its size.

Small marauders

Eventually Roger eased the fish into the net. It weighed no more than 5 lb (2.25 kg), but I could see how well the jacks had adapted for their existence of slash, kill, and run. I caught many more, all around the same size, but the tide was nearing the top of its cycle and the fish were thinning out. We headed off to collect more bait. Snook are fabulous, but you can give me the jacks any time, even the moderately sized ones.

Later that evening, Roger and I decided to try fishing farther up the Indian River, still parallel to the coast. As the sun started to dip, we saw a group of pelicans begin to dive on shoals of bait fish. Surely there had to be predators lurking directly under that tempting fare? Roger stuck a small mullet under his float and cast it so that the current would take the little fish right into the middle of the maelstrom in front of us. We had perfect light for the camera, so I decided to stand by and hope our plan would work.

Mullet-fueled rocket

Suddenly, a fish ripped into Roger's bait and sped off with the current as if there were no one on the other end, so fast and strong was that first run. Roger's medium-weight spinning rod buckled right over and braided line just poured from the reel, but I knew how much he wanted to land a decent jack, and of course I was desperate for a picture of this mullet-fueled rocket. I probably say it too often, but both us of us were astonished by its strength, and I was not even attached to the fish. As it finally came to hand, seemingly exhausted, I could not quite believe that a mere 12 lb (5.5 kg) of jack could lead an angler on so nerve-shattering a dance.

Talking to some local anglers, I learned that jacks of over 40 lb (18 kg) are caught in the Sebastian area. I cannot guess how these can be landed on light tackle, but I have rarely seen an angler as happy as Roger after he hauled in that jack weighing more than the magical 10-lb (4.5-kg) mark. Later on, stopping for one more cup of coffee, we talked of a return trip. Yes, the snook look fantastic and fight like tigers, but those jacks seem to imprint themselves squarely in your consciousness and want to drag you back for more. No true sporting angler could refuse such a call.

ALTERNATIVE LOCATIONS

Great Britain
Shore fishing is practiced around Great Britain. Sandy beaches, such as those of East Anglia, require long-distance casting with small bait. The rocky coasts of Cornwall and Wales require more powerful tackle and bigger bait, and the fishing is closer to the shore.

Namibia
Shore fishing in Namibia is similar to that of the east coast of the US in that you are hunting big fish from golden beaches. The fishing is either just south of Walvis Bay or as far north from there as you wish to go, right up to the border with Angola.

Australia
Many of the shores of this vast continent lend themselves to shore fishing, and the abundance of fish may come as a surprise to anglers from other parts of the world.

TACKLE & TECHNIQUES

How we fished on the Florida coastline depended very much on where we were, for it is always vital to match your fishing method with the situation in front of you. Up north in St. Augustine, Roger and I chose to fish a beach mark that had a very obvious sandbank lying directly in front of us. We suspected that fish would be looking for food in the deeper, turbulent water behind the sandbank. That meant casting out fish bait as far as possible, which is how we tend to shore-fish for English cod.

Long versus short range

Most American anglers fish closer inshore, but on arrival we wanted to compare long-range fishing with the local methods and see which worked better. It turned out that our British beachcasting rods certainly caught fish,

and we were also able to continue fishing when the sea could not be fished at close range and the locals were obliged to find sheltered spots.

A large part of the shore fishing around Florida is done with live bait. Whatever your feelings about using live bait, it is extremely effective and many anglers happily use it to ensure they catch fish. Bait fish are caught with throw-nets; they are then kept alive in buckets of water with battery-powered aerators attached. In the Florida heat you must change the water regularly to keep the bait fish cool and healthy. American tackle shops supply a range of hooks designed especially for livebaiting.

At Sebastian Inlet we followed the example of the local anglers and freelined or float-fished live shrimp, majarra, and sand perch. Freelining is

THROW-NET *(left)* Netting your own bait fish is legal in Florida and ensures a constant supply.

HOOKED UP *(below)* Not everyone will bait with live fish, but they certainly attract predators.

extremely straightforward, but requires absolute concentration. The hook is simply tied onto your mainline or trace, and then the live bait is hooked up and cast out into the tide. The live bait must be allowed to swim freely and naturally, but at the same time you must keep a tight line from the live bait to your rod tip. We found freelining with live shrimp to be an exhilarating form of fishing. The guidelines for freelining also apply to float fishing, although in this case you have the benefit of the float acting as a visual indicator of a bite.

Weighted live bait

We also tried ledgering our live bait in the main flow of the inlet, and this was very successful with the jacks. A variety of onshore sea conditions were affecting our approach to the venue. Success came when we weighted down our bait on the seabed with grip leads, in either the 6-oz (170-g) or the 8-oz (200-g) size. If the water had been calmer, plain leads would have done the job just as well.

GRIP LEAD

Grip wire

Stainless-steel eye

6-oz (170-g) lead weight

SHORE-FISHING MULTIPLIER

Large-capacity spool

Strong frame

Spool-release lever

Star drag

Large handle

BEACH FISHING FOR SNOOK AND JACKS

Rods For the distance casting, use a 4–6-oz (110–170-g) beachcaster from Daiwa, Conoflex, or Century. Heavy spinning rods cope with the jacks and snook.

Reels SLOSH 30s are perfect for the beachcasting work, but use fixed-spool reels with the spinning rods. Make sure the drag system is operating smoothly.

Lines Ultima Red Ice and Tournament Gold were fine on my reels, in breaking strains of 15–30 lb (7–14 kg). For the beach work use 20-lb (9-kg) line and a long, 80-lb (36-kg) shockleader.

Hooks For the beach I used my normal Mustad hooks in sizes 4/0–6/0.

JUTTING OUT (below) A pier brings into range the fish that are feeding beyond the shore breakers.

LIVE SHRIMP (below) Shrimp were our preferred bait when freelining for snook and jacks.

LIVE-BAIT WELLS (below) Frequent water replacement and aeration keep live bait in good condition.

ROCK FISHING FOR IRISH POLLACK

Many rock anglers rate sea bass as the best fish, so why would anyone go for pollack? Admittedly, pollack do not make the finest eating, and bass may fight longer and make some impressive runs. But pollack fishing always has an extra edge of adrenaline. Any minute, a fish might literally smash into your terminal gear and then, before you have a chance to react, crash-dive to the nearest snag with a flick of its powerful tail. Boat anglers will attest that the initial run and dive of the pollack leaves the bass at the starting blocks, but it is when you hook one from the rocks that you really see why they are so highly respected.

Pollack inhabit most of the west-facing coastlines of Britain, including Cornwall, Wales, and Scotland, but the true mecca for serious pollack anglers is the rugged western shore of Ireland. The west coast is subjected to huge Atlantic swells, but on a calm day you can take advantage of some quite spectacular sport. Get away from the crowds and cell phones, deep-spin some sand eel or lures, and lose yourself in the solitude of true rock fishing.

Kilkee

Shannon River

Limerick

IRELAND

"They advised us to try fishing on the rocks outside the harbor, an area that we had ruled out…"

The fishing on the Atlantic coast of Ireland is subject to the weather, more so, perhaps, than most places that I have fished. Six of us had arrived in Cork, southern Ireland, on our way to Kilkee to fish for and photograph the hard-fighting pollack. Imagine our feelings when we got our first view of the port: gray, low skies, driving rain, a howling wind, and a huge swell.

Sea-drenched marks

As we drove toward Kilkee, the skies began to clear. For our base we had chosen this spot on the north side of the Shannon estuary so that, if the weather prevented us from getting out on the rocks, we could move to the estuary for the outstanding ray and bull huss sport. But the famous Irish pollack were our primary goal, so we raced for the coast, only to be met by about the biggest ground swell any of us had ever seen. Under clear blue skies, walls of water were being driven over the rocks and way up the cliffs, swamping any chance we might have had of accessing the open coast marks. We were left with no choice but to head for the Shannon and its thornback ray.

A few days later and the swell was starting to die, but not to the extent of letting us fish exactly where we would have liked. It was time to see whether the locals knew of safer pollack marks. They advised us to try fishing on the rocks outside the harbor, an area that we had ruled out as a waste of time for fishing.

FIRM GRIP The hard-fighting pollack must be taken with a strong, businesslike hook or the angler has little hope of bringing it in.

THE ENVIRONMENT

The west coast of Ireland is exposed to potentially huge swells that pound in directly from the Atlantic. Fishing from the rugged shoreline can be made impossible by the extreme conditions, so it is best to choose a coastal destination that offers quick access to sheltered fishing should the weather turn bad. On our trip, the Shannon estuary was within reach of our main mark at Kilkee.

Temperatures are similar to those of the Shannon estuary (see p.91). Gale-force winds affect the coast most frequently between October and March, reaching their peak in January. Gales are least likely to occur on the coast between June and August.

Rainfall and sunshine Turbulent conditions out in the Atlantic mean that the Irish coast experiences days of heavy rain even in its relatively dry months of April to July. The sunniest months are May and June, but again, individual days can be heavily overcast.

Key fish caught from the rocks at Kilkee are pollack and mackerel.

Other fish at Kilkee are bass and flatfish, which are caught by surf anglers.

Prime time for pollack and other species is between May and September, although there is reasonable fishing year-round.

"All of them were hooked quite literally beneath our feet..."

At last, a chance to get to the pollack. There was a definite sense of excitement in the air as we scrambled over ankle-breaking boulders to the water's edge. The water was smashing over the west-facing rocks not 300 yd (275 m) away, but in this bay we had flat, calm conditions, clear water, and plenty of tide, rocks, and weed. If this had been our home ground we would not have even bothered to fish the mark, but with the open coast out of bounds we were glad of a likely place to find some pollack.

Everybody rushed to set up heavy-duty spinning outfits, then gingerly crept over the weed-strewn rocks to get as close to the water as possible. Polarizing sunglasses enabled us to see below the weedy, rocky, sea wall that stood in front of us. Any pollack in the area would be lurking there; we could see that farther out it was mainly a clean, sandy bottom.

Down by the harbor

During low water at dawn on two successive days we fished this mark and caught numerous pollack, with the best of them around the 7-lb (3-kg) mark; no real monsters, but excellent fish for a mark just outside a town. All of them were hooked quite literally beneath our feet, right at the end of the retrieve. A fair number of fish were lost as they careered into their rocky sanctuary beneath us and stuck fast. Once a pollack has found safety, you need a lot of luck to drag it out, but enough came to our lures and sand-eel bait to convince us first of the quality of the fishing, and second that the open coast, when fishable, would almost certainly provide much bigger fish.

LOW ROCKS The pollack loves tidal rips, rock fissures, and hidden reefs, and the area just outside Kilkee harbor proved a good hunting ground. The dive of a hooked pollack has to be restrained, since the fish use the rocky snags in their defense. My friend, Adam Nicholls, is removing the hook from a pollack's gaping mouth before returning the fish to the water. He also displays a pollack weighing 7 lb (3 kg).

Long Island, New York
The tactics we used on the west coast of Ireland can be applied to catching early-season striped bass from the rockier areas of the Long Island coastline. A lighter approach tends to be used on the island, but the main principles are the same.

Canada
Rockfish, which in Canada can be caught by the bucketload from inshore boats, are also very takeable when fishing from the shore. Like pollack, these colorful fish head straight for their weedy lairs on the bottom when hooked, and you need to apply instant pressure on the rod to keep the line from being snagged. Don't forget that a bear could bump into you while you are doing this—not a problem anglers are likely to face elsewhere.

Northwest France
Much of the Brittany coastline in northwest France has great potential for pollack fishing. The numerous headlands that poke out into the tide are typical habitats for the fish.

"As the tide crept in, we were pushed off our ledges and back toward the town..."

On the rocks, we would cast out the lure or sand eel, wait until it hit the bottom, and then start steadily to retrieve it, always on the alert for a bite. Just when you think nothing is going to happen, a pollack darts out from the weed and smashes into your gear. If the fish runs out and away from you, and your mainline succeeds in cushioning its dive, you are likely to land the fish. But if it heads downward, say goodbye to fish and terminal gear and accept that this is the nature of pollack fishing.

When experienced for the first time, the savage power of a pollack diving is enough to rattle any angler, but do not hesitate; your primary objective is to try to hold the fish and prevent it from reaching safety. Many reels have fantastic built-in drag systems, but these are not much good when up against the pollack. You have to lock your reel solid and offer up a little prayer that your line holds.

A powerful sea

We also fished the morning high waters off diving boards that were screwed to the rocks, something for which a good sense of balance is essential. But we really wanted to have a crack at the open coast. As luck would have it, conditions abated a little more on our last day, giving us the opportunity to fish from a series of ledges out on the coast.

Looking back, I suspect that we should not have fished the mark, for wave after wave was pounding into the rocks and sending rafts of spray flying everywhere. We tore down to the water's edge, flung out the lures, then raced back to relative safety and started retrieving, but really we didn't stand a chance. You need to be as near to vertical as possible over a fish

to stop its dive, but we were unable to stay at the edge for any length of time. A few small fish were landed, but big fish were lost when they dived and rid themselves of the hook.

Still, rock fishing seldom gets much more dramatic than this, and ultimately I was quite happy just to sit and be mesmerized by the battering of the sea. There were fish out there, we were reasonably safe, but really we knew that we were fighting a losing battle and that defeat was inevitable. As the tide crept in, we were pushed off our ledges and back toward the town, where the waters were calmer and the fish somewhat easier to catch.

To fish another day

This was the first time we had fished in Irish waters, and we went with an open mind. Our local contact in Kilkee, when out in his boat less than 20 yd (18 m) off the west-facing rocks, regularly caught fish of 10 lb (4.5 kg) or more, but obviously that was when the swell was a lot more conducive to fishing. Ireland is part of northern Europe and so the weather was bound to vary—there is nothing the angler can do about it. Our talk on the journey back home seldom strayed from the fishing we had experienced, but we knew that we had barely scratched the surface of the potential fishing around Kilkee.

We hope to return to Kilkee, when maybe the waters will be kinder. Perhaps the conditions are not critical, for we had discovered that safe pollack fishing can be found in almost any weather. There is also the ray sport in the nearby Shannon estuary. The urge to return is hard to resist, especially with the promise of larger pollack on the open coast.

ATLANTIC SWELL A diving board gave us a vantage point vertically above where the pollock were lurking at the foot of the cliff. Effective teamwork is required to land open-coast pollack; one angler battles the fish and winds it in, while the other climbs down to net the fish. My friend, Rob Wheaton, certainly admired his doughty, rock-scarred pollack.

SAFE FISHING FROM ROCKY SHORES

HIGH EXPOSURE Never risk your life to catch fish. A location above spectacular spray may be quite safe, but make sure you understand the conditions before settling in. Always stand in a place where you can focus on your fishing, not on your foothold. Fishing on broken terrain is safe only if you are certain that the sea will not suddenly force you to flee.

Flat, sandy beaches might seem the most perfect fishing locations, being the safest and most easily accessible places from which to catch fish. But often the best sport occurs at the out-of-the-way rock marks where few people tread; you are likely to find the best fish where the water is deeper, the tides faster, and the seabed broken and varied. However, rock fishing is a specialized activity with some risks, and you need to consider how to go about it. Safety measures need not be complicated, so put in the effort and you will reap the rewards.

Footwear

Typically, a rocky coastline consists of steep, sometimes towering, headlands interspersed with sand or pebble beaches and river estuaries. Climbing down to the more inaccessible marks can be laborious and difficult. Arriving at the mark, you may have to move around on slippery, uneven surfaces while you fish. Every angler therefore should consider which footwear would best suit these conditions.

Many anglers choose ankle-high, thick-soled walking boots, available from outdoor equipment stores, for use on rocks. These are extremely comfortable and hard-wearing, and provide a good grip on rocky surfaces.

On wet, slippery rocks, move with extreme caution, whatever you are wearing on your feet. Test the grip of hiking boots on wet rocks before putting your trust in them. Rubber boots and thigh waders are best avoided on all but the simplest rock marks, but chest waders incorporating felt- or cleated-soled wading boots provide fantastic grip. Fly-fishing shops are a good source of quality waders.

Carrying equipment

On rocky coastlines it is often necessary to carry equipment some distance from your transportation to the mark. The equipment can be bulky, especially for long cold-weather sessions. It is essential to spread the load across your back and shoulders and keep your body nicely balanced for walking and climbing. A

large-capacity backpack is best. Before setting off, pack your backpack with your tackle, clothing, lighting, food and drink, bait, and so on, spreading the load evenly. Make sure the pack feels comfortable to wear, and adjust its shoulder and waist straps accordingly. Carry your rods, gaff, and rod-stand in a special bag, ideally one that goes over your shoulders and leaves your hands free.

Ropes

Occasionally, ropes may be helpful in getting to inaccessible places, but do not even think of using them if you do not feel totally safe doing so. I never get near the point of rappeling, but I might hit a big metal spike into the ground, attach a rope, and use that to get me down to where I want to fish. Ropes are not for the fainthearted, though, and it should go without saying that only a fool would use a rope while alone, especially at night.

Lighting

Much of my fishing is carried out at night, when certain fish are moving inshore to feed. Night fishing carries its own risks but is often the only option. The most essential piece of equipment is a good-quality head lantern. I could not imagine fishing without it—

wherever you look, the beam of light follows. A head lantern provides a strong beam while you are walking, climbing, and landing fish, and it leaves both hands free. Most types are powered by rechargeable batteries that provide more than enough light for a fishing session.

The weather and the sea

Success in rock fishing is closely governed by the weather and the tides, as indeed is all sea fishing. Fish respond to certain wind directions and strengths, and also to water conditions. The more you fish, the more attention you need to pay to weather forecasts. Slowly but surely, you learn how the weather will affect where you hope to fish, as well as how the fish are going to behave and feed. All possible prior knowledge is hugely valuable for safe and successful rock fishing. On the mark, go with your gut instinct and learn to trust it.

The rock fisherman must always keep an eye trained on the sea, constantly watching for signs of danger. The day you relax too much is the day the sea rears up and gives you a nasty and possibly fatal lesson. There are times when we need to fish in extremely rough conditions, but no fish is ever worth a life. The successful rock angler knows that the sea is always in control, and you can never trust the sea.

TACKLE & TECHNIQUES

Robustness is the key factor in pollack fishing—you can forget the subtle ways of mulleting. Think more of giving yourself every chance of hanging onto that initial crash-dive, and then of having to wrench the fish from its intended destination. Some anglers use conger-strength tackle to catch big, bottom-feeding pollack, but that does not give you a true sense of how pollack fight.

Instead, think in terms of medium-to-heavy spinning of sand eels or lures, and even float fishing live bait when the conditions and territory allow. For deep-spinning bait or lures, let a plain 3–4-oz (85–115-g) weight slide on the shockleader, stopped by a couple of beads and the swivel (the swivel is the core of every trace, acting as a connector and preventing line twist). Keep the trace to about 36 in (90 cm) in length.

Mount a defrosted sand eel head first, bind it onto the hook with elasticated thread, and cast it out. Let the rig hit the bottom lightly and immediately start a steady retrieve (the same applies if you are using a jelly worm, artificial eel, or lure). When fishing close to the seabed, there is always a risk of losing end tackle among the rocks and weeds, but once you get the "feel" of the depth, you are less likely to be constantly snagging the line. You can also fish at a lesser depth if you find that the fish are feeding away from the bottom.

In areas where you have the right tide to keep a 3–4-oz (85–115-g) float moving, try fishing live sand eels or ragworm on the end of a 30-lb (14-kg) trace. As to the depth to set the bait, it is usually the deeper the better, but experiment and see what works bests.

JELLY WORMS *(below left)* Sometimes pollack will grab brightly colored jelly worms.

SAFETY NET *(below)* A net is an essential item for landing the bigger pollack safely.

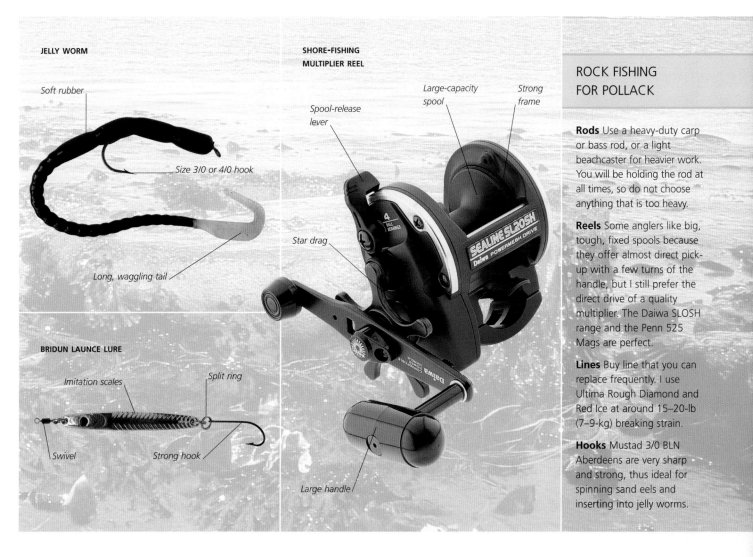

JELLY WORM

Soft rubber

Size 3/0 or 4/0 hook

Long, waggling tail

BRIDUN LAUNCE LURE

Imitation scales

Split ring

Swivel

Strong hook

**SHORE-FISHING
MULTIPLIER REEL**

Spool-release lever

Large-capacity spool

Strong frame

Star drag

Large handle

ROCK FISHING FOR POLLACK

Rods Use a heavy-duty carp or bass rod, or a light beachcaster for heavier work. You will be holding the rod at all times, so do not choose anything that is too heavy.

Reels Some anglers like big, tough, fixed spools because they offer almost direct pick-up with a few turns of the handle, but I still prefer the direct drive of a quality multiplier. The Daiwa SLOSH range and the Penn 525 Mags are perfect.

Lines Buy line that you can replace frequently. I use Ultima Rough Diamond and Red Ice at around 15–20-lb (7–9-kg) breaking strain.

Hooks Mustad 3/0 BLN Aberdeens are very sharp and strong, thus ideal for spinning sand eels and inserting into jelly worms.

FALSE LIKENESS *(below)* The 1¾-oz (50-g) Bridun Launce can be a highly effective pollack lure.

EEL BAIT *(bottom left and below)* The pollack is highly adept at grabbing a spun eel and diving hard.

SURF CASTING FOR SHARKS ON THE NAMIBIAN COAST

I f you enjoy beach fishing, the Atlantic coast of Namibia, famously called the Skeleton Coast, must be among the finest destinations in the world. Years ago, when I was first shown pictures of huge sharks caught direct from those West African beaches, I could only goggle in disbelief. Without a boat to follow the shark, how would you put line back on the reel other than by sheer, blunt-headed determination?

I was about to find out. After a sleepless, adrenaline-fueled flight to Windhoek and an awe-inspiring truck ride across the Namibian desert, my group and I joined our guide in Walvis Bay. Together we trekked northward, following a shore that lay eerily deserted but for pelicans and seals. Standing on that empty beach, it was disturbing to think that big predators were patrolling the waters before us— bronze whaler sharks, spotted gully sharks, and hound sharks. There were also kabeljou (kob) and steenbras, both offering potent fishing in their own right. But it was the bronzies that fascinated me; this was my first chance to hook a shark from a beach, rather than from a boat.

"I just wanted a monster shark on the end of my line and the chance to bring it in..."

To the non-angler, fishing must seem much the same the world over—simply small fish or large fish, caught in a variety of locations. But to those of us for whom angling is a personal obsession, nothing could be further from the truth. Thus it was that, although the Namibian beaches offered fishing for kob and smaller sharks, my first goal was to catch a "proper" shark off the shore. To be specific, it had to be a bronze whaler shark, otherwise known to the locals as the copper shark, or "bronzy."

We had driven to a section of the beach that our guide, Terence Clark, assured us held enough color in the water to bring in the bronze whalers very tight to the shoreline. It should be said that, to the outsider, every bit of beach tends to look the same as the next. The Skeleton Coast is certainly unspoiled, vast, and uncrowded, but you need the expert services of a very knowledgeable guide to find the fish. To Terence's informed eyes, every eddy and swirl of the water was betraying fish-holding features, and now the turbulent water in front of us apparently held sharks. I found that the empty beach, and the knowledge that big sharks were cruising within easy reach, wreaked havoc with my imagination. I was buzzing with fear-edged adrenaline. I didn't care a bit whether the first one would defeat me; I just wanted a monster shark on the end of my line and the chance to bring it in.

Waiting for a thunderbolt

Soon I was standing calf-deep in the Atlantic Ocean, 14 ft (4.25 m) of beachcaster cradled in my arms, impatiently searching for any sign of a shark. But not a movement of the rod tip, not even a sniff at the bait. Excitement and apprehension fought within me; this would be a much bigger fish than anything I had caught before. Just how powerful could it possibly be? The reel's drag was set so tight that, should a bronzy take the bait, I was half expecting to be swept literally off my feet.

OMINOUS FIN If you are not accustomed to sharks in your home waters, the sight of "your" first shark swirling in the shallows will live with you forever. The thrill is indescribable.

THE ENVIRONMENT

The Skeleton Coast is famous for its shipwrecks. It includes all of Namibia's coastline and continues 125 miles (200 km) north into Angola. Beach fishing takes place just south and to the north of Walvis Bay. Also to the north is the Skeleton Coast National Park, which was created in 1971 and is partly managed as a wilderness reserve.

Temperatures in the area are moderate in the summer months, and there is usually a cooling onshore breeze, especially during the afternoon. It is seldom hotter than 86°F (30°C)—much cooler than the desert inland. Winter temperatures can be hotter—in excess of 104°F (40°C)—an effect of hot easterly winds.

Rainfall and sunshine Annual rainfall is light, occurring in widely separated periods of drizzle. Sunshine can be obscured by dense ocean fog.

Key fish include bronze whalers (also called copper sharks), spotted gully sharks, hound sharks, cow sharks, and kabeljou (kob).

Other fish caught from the sandy beaches include steenbras, kingklip, and small catfish. Galjoen and blacktail are found in rocky areas of the coast.

Prime time for sharks is from October until April, although they can be caught year-round. Kob are best fished for between September and March.

"Really it was all down to me and the shark, and nobody else..."

I was twirling the line between my fingers and attempting to keep calm when, out of the blue, the rod tip slammed over. An unseen predator had ripped into my bait. In one split second, with Terence's cry of "Strike, strike!" ringing in my ears, I pointed the rod toward the bait and then tried to set the hook. What happened next was one of those unforgettable moments, shot through with pure elation mixed with absolute terror. Much as I would like to think that my reaction looked like two drawn-out seconds of pure angling skill, I suspect that, to a seasoned sharker like Terence, it had every appearance of blind panic.

One-to-one combat

I instinctively went for two quick strikes, but on the second one I could not actually lift the rod right back to the horizontal. The "thing" on the end of my line had suddenly realized its predicament and was now ripping line from my reel at an incredible speed. Most alarming of all was the ease with which this shark was taking line against the tight drag of my reel.

I tried hard to hang on and get properly focused on the matter at hand, battling to shake off a kind of paralysis caused by both wonder and horror. It occurred to me that nobody had ever trained me for this; this time I had no experienced boat skipper following the shark and helping me to put back line on the rapidly emptying reel. This was what every angler dreams of: to be hooked up to an express train of a fish; advice was available if I asked for it, but really it was all down to me and the shark, and nobody else.

SHARK ALERT On the Namibian coast we fished in the same way as the local fishermen: standing, holding the rod at all times, and preparing for a long fight. When you see a shark in the shallows and seemingly beaten, each wave may yet bring the possibility of another bid to escape. Gaffing a shark in the dorsal fin does not harm the fish, and all sharks are returned to the water uninjured. As a newcomer to the scene, words could not convey how happy I was to beach my first bronzy.

"This living, breathing shark lies beached, as exhausted as you are from the fight…"

Fighting the bronzy on that day was nothing short of incredible. Many of the fish in my home waters give good fights and produce wonderful moments, but I would never describe fighting those fish as being physically tiring. Never before had I been connected to a fish that made my muscles scream in pain: the power is unforgettable, as is the sheer anger of the shark as it repeatedly runs out to sea in its quest to shed the hook or empty your reel.

A waking dream

Imagine seeing that shark surfacing for the first time, perhaps 50 yd (45 m) out, and cruising up and down, parallel to the beach. With the fish still to be landed, you fear that your strength will fail you, yet somehow you find in yourself the angler's willpower to keep fighting. Gradually you haul the beast into the shallows, where your guide safely beaches it. You try to stand up, collapse, then stand once more and run down the beach to where this living, breathing shark lies beached, as exhausted as you are from the fight. Gingerly, you hold the jaws open and retrieve what looks, in scale, like a very small and ineffectual lump of hook, and then you sink down to the sand and admire one of nature's most efficient machines.

Returned to the sea

Elation mixed with absolute relief washed over me as I gazed upon my first bronzy, but better was the feeling when I gently pulled the shark back into the water and watched the huge tail power the fish back out into the depths. It was an eerie thought that my first big shark was but one of many, for there really are huge numbers of them off the Skeleton Coast.

On this trip, like most fishermen visiting Namibia from overseas, we were concerned primarily with the predators lurking within casting range of the beaches. In addition to the bronzies are numerous other species, including the spotted gully sharks. I would guess that most anglers would find the fight with a spottie quite spectacular enough and would quite happily fish for them all day long. The

CASTING OUT With large fish such as sharks, kob, and steenbras swimming close in to the shore, you never know what your bait will attract.

...

Namibian anglers, on the other hand, are mostly interested in edible fish; the sharks are not eaten. While I personally found it almost impossible to drag myself away from the bronzies, there is also good fishing for the edible kabeljou (kob) and steenbras, and it is a shame to ignore these magnificent fish.

Kob fishing

The kob is a species that tends to swim in large shoals off Namibia, moving in and out of the surf plateaus as it hunts for food. When they are still growing, kob look a little like sea bass, but once they have exceeded maybe 20 lb (9 kg) they seem to grow out sideways instead of lengthwise, attaining deep bellies and looking very unique as a result. Kob average perhaps 10 lb (4.5 kg) in weight, but far bigger specimens are regularly landed.

I have not encountered the steenbras, the other game species that is caught specifically from the sandy beaches, but know that they are highly prized, looking something like big sea bream. The bigger steenbras have a reputation for fierce fighting but, like many fish, they are available only during their season.

KOB TROPHIES The kob, an edible fish, was caught in various sizes off the shore, but the biggest we saw was the specimen held here by a local man named Spyker *(bottom left)*. Its weight was 58 lb (26 kg). Since we were some distance from any facilities, our vehicle and trailer served as base camp.

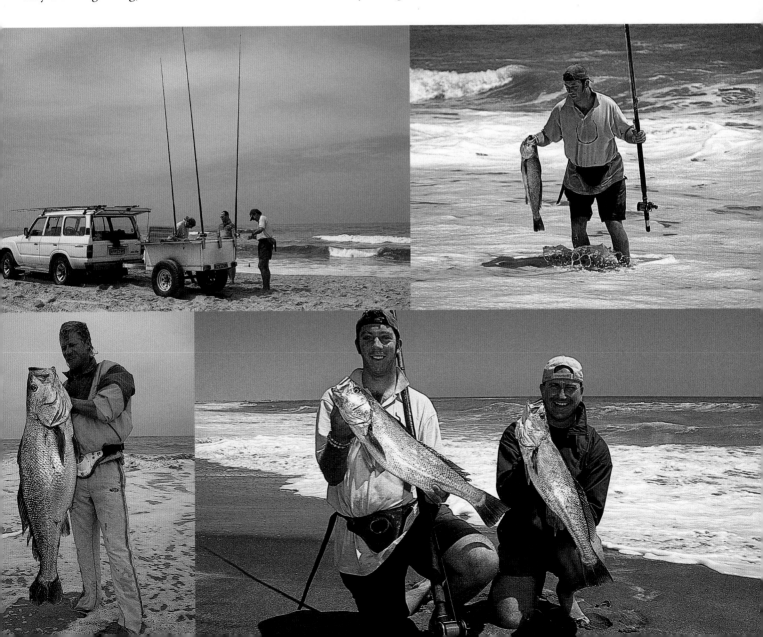

BIG FISH IN THE SEA Spotted gully sharks were put in the shade somewhat by the presence of the bigger bronzies (*bottom right*), which we regarded as the top trophy. Sharks and edibles are not the only fish; the waters also held a local species of stingray. I was extremely happy with my 14-lb (6-kg) kob, although such a fish is not big enough to turn any heads on the beach.

"Like a madman, I wound in as fast as I could to make contact with the unseen presence..."

One magical morning we trekked up to Mile 108 (the nearly featureless shore is signposted in this way) to fish for kob. The surf was pounding in and the beach around us was eerily deserted; we felt as though we were on the edge of the world. There we cast our bait onto the calmer sandbanks and plateaus, where Terence assured us the kob preferred to feed. There was nothing to do but stand there, waiting hopefully for a bite.

Landing the first kob

For an hour nothing took the bait, but Terence did not want to move. Conditions looked ideal to him and we had to trust our guide's judgment. He was waiting for the tide to start ebbing. At around 10 am my rod slammed over and then everything just dropped slack. Like a madman, I wound in as fast as I could to make contact with the unseen presence. At last the rod hooped over and I knew that connection had been made. My silver bar raced one way and then the other, parallel to each surf line, but after a while my pressure told on the fish and finally it submitted to being brought in.

Now, I could not have been any happier with my first, 14-lb (6-kg) kob. That was a big fish to me, but in Namibia they continue to grow much bigger. We caught several more kob that day but, as I often find, it was my first catch of the species that had ingrained itself on my mind. Somehow, a first catch seems to get fixed in memory like a photograph, almost trapped in the time that you caught it.

Later, casting out onto a sandy plateau between breakers, we chanced upon what was obviously a large shoal of kob feeding hard.

Our method was straightforward: cast out, tighten the line, and then expect to be hit. The fish either charges off and hooks itself against the grip lead, or races in toward you. Either way, you strive to keep the line tight and get the fish in; then you grab it, unhook it, and race to the truck for some more bait.

This kind of fishing does not last long because all the time you are losing the tide. Anglers must take advantage of the brief, frenzied feeding spells. As quickly as possible, we replaced our bait and cast out again. I found myself wondering whether all beaches had once fished as well as this, before the fish succumbed to commercial pressure.

Losing the shoal of fish, we jumped into the trucks and headed off to find some more bronzies. Although already fatigued by our morning of hectic kob fishing, we wanted to spend more hours attached to big, runaway fish. No one would disagree that anglers sleep the sleep of the exhausted in Namibia.

Big, and bigger still

The last time I was on the beach, a local guide, called Spyker, came to show us a huge lump of a kob that he had recently caught. I took a few pictures of the 58-lb (26-kg) monster, but no photograph really does justice to these impressive fish. That being so, I was later shown photographs of a kob that was hooked, beached, and released by an angler who was beach fishing much farther north than where we had been. Everyone agreed that a conservative estimation of its weight would be around the 200-lb (90-kg) mark. Unbelievably, my photograph of Spyker's fish barely shows how big these kob can grow.

ALTERNATIVE LOCATIONS

Angola
This country lies directly north of Namibia and its inshore coastal waters are inhabited by many sharks. As well as bronzies there are hammerhead sharks so big that they make the bronzies seem modest in size. Angola is only now opening up as a fishing destination.

South Africa
Around Durban it is possible to take big sharks from the beaches and the large breakwater (they used to catch huge great whites off there), as well as various species of ray.

Mozambique
Big bronze whalers, bull sharks, and the beautiful eagle ray can be taken from the beach. Again, this fishing is only just opening up to tourists, but guides and tackle are available. Make sure you travel with a reputable company, for this is very new ground.

Queensland, Australia
Fraser Island, lying 125 miles (200 km) north of Brisbane, is known for the abnormally large sharks offshore. The fishing demands boat tackle and is done from platforms built onto piers and trucks. Fish of over 600 lb (270 kg) have been landed.

Florida Keys
Nurse and lemon sharks, as well as various species of stingray, are easily taken from the numerous jetties and piers. Fish at night with either heavy boat equipment or beachcasting gear, and groundbait heavily.

TACKLE & TECHNIQUES

Any tackle used to catch sharks must be strong, simple, and unfussy. In Namibia this does not mean heavy boat-fishing equipment; the gear used is no heavier than any beachcasting or rock-fishing tackle. The Namibian guides are anglers after my own heart, for they eschew fancy rigs and setups in favor of balanced reels, rods, and terminal tackle that have only one goal; to get fish onto the beach with maximum efficiency.

Hand-worked reels

Hooked sharks run fast, hard, and often a long way out to sea, so the Namibians have large reels that hold a lot of line. Unusually, they tend to remove the built-in magnetic or mechanical braking systems from their reels and simply thumb them when casting. I am used to a braked reel and find theirs too "lively"

and hard to handle. They, on the other hand, find it strange that an angler would ever want to brake the reel. The reels tend to be placed down toward the butt of the rod, and butt-pads are always strapped on; that way, the maximum pressure can be exerted on a shark without the rod bruising the angler.

Sharks have razor-sharp teeth and rip through mono lines with ease. I expected very heavy wire traces to be used, but in general the wire was only 150-lb (70-kg) nylon-coated wire, rigged with a swivel and a pair of 9/0 Mustad Kendall hooks. Bronzed hooks tend to be used because, should they break off, the remnant will quickly rust out of the shark's mouth.

Bait for bronze shark includes heads of mackerel, kob, and snook, sections of mackerel and mullet, and "sausages"

ROD REST *(below)* In Namibia, rods were always held; only at lunch did we put them down.

TRUSSED TIDBIT *(below)* In this tied bait for kob is some foam rubber to lift it just off the bottom.

made from the liver and gills of spotted gully sharks and sand sharks. Mullet heads are good for spotties, and pilchard heads and sections, together with squid and white mussel, for kob. I expected the shark bait to be huge, to match their appetites, but it is not; large bait would be impossible to cast, and also the Namibians want the shark to be able to pick up the offering quickly.

Depending on sea conditions and the tide, plain and grip leads are used to get the bait down to the targeted fish, When kob fishing, a small piece of foam is often wound to the bait to keep it just off the bottom and away from weeds.

Local expertise

As for the casting, you have to see the Namibian guides at work to believe it. With no brake in the reel and heavy mainline, they effortlessly alternate throwing out the bait with darting in and out of the surf. They make it look very simple, but how they control those big reels is a mystery to me.

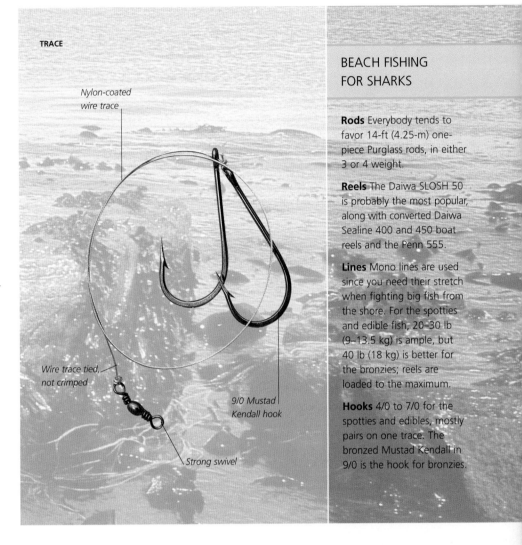

TRACE

Nylon-coated wire trace

Wire trace tied, not crimped

9/0 Mustad Kendall hook

Strong swivel

BEACH FISHING FOR SHARKS

Rods Everybody tends to favor 14-ft (4.25-m) one-piece Purglass rods, in either 3 or 4 weight.

Reels The Daiwa SLOSH 50 is probably the most popular, along with converted Daiwa Sealine 400 and 450 boat reels and the Penn 555.

Lines Mono lines are used since you need their stretch when fighting big fish from the shore. For the spotties and edible fish, 20–30 lb (9–13.5 kg) is ample, but 40 lb (18 kg) is better for the bronzies; reels are loaded to the maximum.

Hooks 4/0 to 7/0 for the spotties and edibles, mostly pairs on one trace. The bronzed Mustad Kendall in 9/0 is the hook for bronzies.

KOB BAIT (below) A grip lead is used to anchor this pennel-rigged pilchard bait to the bottom.

TWIN HOOKS (below) Pennel-rigged hooks are built into the fishmeat bait used for sharks.

ON THE
OPEN SEA

"You have to trust in your skill, and that of the skipper, to get your lures or bait in among fish that will respond to them..."

There is no feeling comparable to that of stepping on board a boat with your fishing tackle and heading out to sea. Whether you plan to fish close inshore or cover a great distance, you are trusting in a weather forecast and in either your own boating skills or those of a professional skipper. Few anglers can honestly claim, when dry land has dipped below the horizon, that being on the open sea does not add a frisson of adventure to the day.

Sea fishing tends to divide into two types. In the first, the boat heads out to tightly defined areas of sea where the fish are believed to be, and the fishing moves from one such location to another. In the second, the boat heads for a wider, looser area, and chum (strong-smelling bait of fishmeat, blood, and oil) is introduced into the water to attract the fish to the boat. Chum can prove irresistible to many mid- and surface-water feeders.

My first sea-fishing trip took place in the flats and coastal waters surrounding the famous Florida Keys. What struck me as amazing was the extreme shallowness of the water; grounding your small, flat-bottomed boat at speed is a real hazard. The water is also very clear. When normally your quarry is seldom visible, except for the occasional shark fin or breaching shoal, it comes as a real shock to see big ray gliding off the flats, and sharks vying for position at the back of your boat. Strangely, in Florida few people set out to target the sharks and rays of the backcountry, for these offer very exciting fishing. Given that you can easily see your fish when it comes in to take the bait, you can expect to have some very big thrills.

My second trip, wreck fishing over the hulks of ships lying at the bottom of the English Channel, was an example of closely targeted sport, where the boat is used to home in on the fish like a well aimed dart.

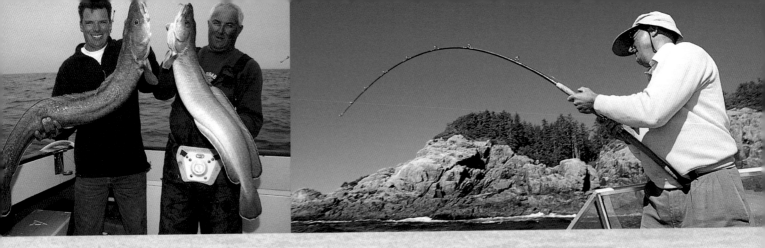

The skipper uses local knowledge and sophisticated technology to zoom in on the underwater wrecks, which hold large colonies of fish and their predators. Since the structures lie at depths of more than 200 ft (60 m), wreck fishing is always done blind. Lowering your gear from the pitching boat onto the unseen mass of rusting metal below, you have to trust in your skill, and that of the skipper, to get your lures or bait in among the fish that will respond to them.

Into the vast Pacific

On my next trip, punching out into a rolling Pacific swell off the west coast of Vancouver Island could not have felt more different to wrecking in the gloomy British winter, or racing around the Florida Keys in high-speed boats. At dawn the skippers would start up the engines and we would head out of Barkley Sound and on to the open ocean. Our target fish were the big salmon that congregate in the ocean prior to moving up the rivers to spawn, and the last of the season's big halibut. The Canadian salmon shoals were a revelation, with coho salmon intercepting our bait as it sank down toward the deeper-swimming, bigger spring salmon, and fighting furiously as they were reeled in toward the boat.

My final trip in this book was to the feeding grounds of the porbeagle shark that lie north of Cornwall, southwest England. Like the lemon sharks we had caught in Florida, these razor-toothed, point-nosed fish were tempted toward us with chum. The idea is that the sharks find the bait first, but sometimes they swim straight in and grab the bags of chum from underneath your nose. Boat fishing brings you face to face with some of the biggest game fish, and the ensuing battles, to and fro over the open water, are among the most exhilarating and testing in fishing.

FISHING FOR SHARKS AND TARPON IN FLORIDA

Nothing prepares the first-time visitor for the unique fishing environment that lies south of Miami in the Florida Keys. European anglers do come across inshore shark fishing, but to see sharks roaming in such shallow, clear waters is quite alarming. In Florida you have only to put on a pair of polarizing sunglasses and the whole marine environment is there to view. It was a shock to see stingrays the size of car hoods gliding around with sharks, barracudas, and numerous other species, all seemingly without a care in the world.

Although most people think of the Keys as a mecca for bonefish and the mighty tarpon, my bunch of intrepid anglers were no less interested in fishing the extensive flats of the backcountry for shark and ray. No problem. Fishing is valued as a high-income activity in Florida, and the marinas are full of charter boats and private fishing vessels, not to mention the vast tackle marts. Conservation is practiced and the waters kept in pristine condition, ensuring that anglers go back again and again.

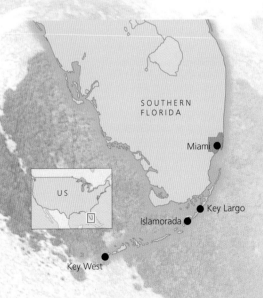

A SIMPLE RIG Sometimes the simplest bait presentation is the most effective. Here a small bait fish is hooked and ready to cast out into the warm water.

"You can look over the side and identify the ominous-looking shapes below..."

A few hours' drive from Miami, our base in the Florida Keys was Islamorada, where we had rented open boats from Caloosa Cove Marina. The first morning dawned very hot and still, and the moment the boats were fueled up we raced out to our first mark. On board we had calamari squid and blocks of chum, which we were assured would catch us all the pinfish live bait we would need. Soon we had plenty of black margate (black bream) in the live-wells, ready to be called upon.

A monstrous stingray

Within 10 minutes of anchoring at our next mark, slightly offshore, my guide, Graeme Pullen, hooked a vast slab of a stingray, but it steadfastly refused to lift off the bottom. Half an hour of concerted pressure did nothing, so I took a turn, thinking this fish was surely at my mercy. Yet 20 more minutes of sustained effort still failed to budge the fish. We could see it lying on the bottom, sucking into the sand, while the rod was close to breaking point and our arms were shaking from the exertion. Suffice to say it was huge, well over 200 lb (90 kg); I silently cursed that stingray for not coming up and showing us its sheer size.

We spent a lot of our time in Florida fishing what is called the backcountry. It was quite something to see and catch fish in such shallow water. Weaving between the shallow flats are gullies and channels that you need to follow in order to avoid grounding the boat. The professional guides zoom around this complex terrain at incredible speeds; their heads must contain comprehensive maps of exactly where to go, and, more importantly, where not to go. That is the kind of skill that grows as it is passed down through generations, honed by countless days spent out on the water, navigating, fishing, and guiding in the shifting marine environment.

During our stay we anchored at a number of the channels, where we threw out the chum to attract the sharks. The channels varied from 15–20 yd (14–18 m) wide and were only 6½–8 ft (2–2.5 m) deep; the flats to either side would be around 2 ft (0.6 m) deep. As our trails of mashed fish mixed with oil drifted off with the tide, fish would pick up the scent and home in on our bait. Black silhouettes would appear on the bottom or puffs of sand would signal the arrival of a fish. Usually you can look over the side and identify the ominous-looking shapes below.

It was not always easy fishing. Sometimes we had plenty of big fish behind the boat and then, for some inexplicable reason, they would stubbornly refuse to feed. Sharks seldom lay off feeding for long, however, and usually it was simply a matter of waiting until one of them turned, swept in, and took the bait.

THE ENVIRONMENT

The Florida Keys are a chain of more than 100 tropical islands surrounded by shallow sand and grass flats that cover 1,034 sq miles (2,678 sq km). Water depths in the flats may be as little as 6 in (15 cm). Good areas for fishing include Key West, the Lower Keys, Marathon, Islamorada, and Key Largo.

Temperatures range from an average high of 89.2°F (31.8°C) in August to an average low of 65.0°F (18.3°C) in January.

Rainfall and sunshine The wettest months in the flats are September and June; the driest and sunniest months are March and April.

Key fish include sharks, giant tarpon—catches range from 50 to150 lb (23 to 68 kg), although fish of up to 200 lb (90 kg) are landed—smaller local tarpon (called silver kings), and bonefish.

Other fish that can be caught in the flats include permit, redfish, snook, speckled trout, snapper, dorado, sailfish, tuna, grouper, and barracuda.

Prime time for tarpon fishing is mid-April to mid-July. However, most target species, including sharks, can be found in the flats year-round.

"A group of long, sleek lemon sharks was moving toward us..."

On our third day we sailed directly above an inert nurse shark. We then turned the boat, anchored, and hooked it within five minutes. It really was as simple as that. As the fish charged off over the flats, it seemed more like a giant bull huss than a shark on the end of my line. The fight consisted of one long, powerful run and then a series of awesome, extremely aggressive head-shakes that sent vibrations right down the mainline and through my forearms. At last we very gingerly unhooked the defeated nurse shark and loosely estimated its weight to be around 60–80 lb (27–36 kg), although it was the experience rather than the size that mattered to me.

American sizes

In Florida you can head a little offshore to find bigger nurses of 200 lb (90 kg) or more; but inshore you still have a chance to pass right over a fish and set about catching it, as we did. If European anglers could catch bull huss that grew to that sort of size, the rock fishing would definitely step up a gear.

That same day we tried a fresh mark. Over the stern went the chum bags and downtide went the bait for the fish we hoped would turn up. A few stingray moved around on the nearby flats and determinedly kept their distance, but within an hour of our chum slick starting its dirty work, a group of long, sleek lemon sharks was moving toward us. There is nothing quite as amazing, and I might also say disturbing, as seeing sharks moving freely just by you, hunting for the source of the blood in the water, and hopefully your bait, too. These lemon sharks were gliding just below the surface, twisting and turning as they moved through the chum slick, seemingly vying for position. Moving as fast as we could, we rigged up fish baits suspended under balloon floats and sent them out to the waiting sharks.

STREAMLINED PREDATOR The lemon shark has long, sleek lines, a shape that has evolved for hunting and gliding in shallow waters. Our guide, Graeme, is using a balanced 30-lb (14-kg) class setup to reel in first a lemon shark and then a stingray. Graeme has been tagging sharks for years, and has done so with this powerful lemon shark; much can be learned from returned tags.

ALTERNATIVE
LOCATIONS

Cuba
While a lot of anglers are
getting excited about the
quality of Cuban inshore
fly-fishing for bonefish and
other species, my ears prick
up at the mention of all the
rays and sharks that pass
their boats. At times the
bottom can be literally
carpeted with stingrays.
Sport fish hooked on the fly
are regularly seized from the
line by marauding sharks.

Cape York, Australia
Cape York, the northernmost
tip of Queensland, has a
vast expanse of flats crawling
with fish of all descriptions,
including rays, sharks, and
some of the finest saltwater
fly-fishing available.

Bahamas
The flats around these
islands are world-famous
for their fishing. Perhaps the
most sought-after quarry is
the bonefish, but many
other species haunt the
shallow, crystal-clear waters.
Inevitably, there are plenty
of marauding sharks to prey
on the shoals of fish.

"My fish gave me a 40-minute lesson on why tarpon are held in such high esteem..."

The biggest of the sharks did hook up for an instant and started to peel line from the reel at missile speed, but all too quickly it shed the hook and fled to sanctuary. We realized that our time was running out; we were losing the all-essential tidal flow, and consequently the current was no longer carrying the strong smell of chum to the fish. Like shadows, the sharks were leaving to pursue other kinds of prey far off in the vast backcountry waters.

Given that they had so much ground over which to feed, we were feeling immensely privileged to have attracted so many of them to the boat; just to have induced one solid hookup seemed enough. On later visits to the mark, we successfully hooked several lemons; the fights were full of speed, tight turns, and angry teeth trying to lacerate the wire traces.

Power and resolution
On one occasion, an angler who had been fishing with us, Matt Hunwick, hooked a big lemon shark in extremely shallow water. Matt braced himself for over an hour on the bow while his 250-lb (115-kg) lemon towed us this way and that, from our anchor point in the channel right over the top of some waist-high flats, and still the fish was not beaten. Perhaps five times we leaned over and saw the shark come right to the side of the boat, almost presenting itself for landing, before powerfully surging off again over the mud and silt. When the fish at last was clearly beaten, after perhaps an hour and a half of prolonged give and take, Matt and Graeme decided to get into the water and unhook the awesome creature, actually cradling it while it regained full strength (see p.133, bottom right).

By now we were itching to tackle some of Florida's legendary tarpon. In the early evening we revisited the pinfish mark, then set the boat to drift with breeze and tide. This kind of fishing is surprisingly simple, for all we were doing was drifting live pinfish away from the boat under cork floats. All was peaceful until, about 10 minutes from commencing the drift, something tried to wrench the rod from my grasp: bang, slam—but then nothing on the hook. I played out new bait, then lay back on the bow to take in the setting sun and the silence, with the rod now very firmly in my grasp and my heart pounding with pure and unadulterated adrenaline. But surely that had been my one and only chance?

Runaway torpedo
Within the hour something hit my bait again and line started melting off the multiplier at a frightening speed. I was under the strictest instructions from Graeme not to strike, but that would have been impossible anyway with the suddenness of the hit and the power of the initial run. Jumping twice in quick succession clear out of the water, my fish gave me a 40-minute lesson on why tarpon are held in such high esteem. "Powerful" is too feeble a word to describe these fish; the sight of about 140 lb (64 kg) of glistening, heavily scaled tarpon ready for unhooking is unforgettable.

With shaking and fumbling hands, I rattled off some pictures of my captive. You expect a shark to be a big fish, but how do you take in a 6½-ft (2-m) giant herring? I am resolved to catch more tarpon, and I know there are a few places where they can be taken from the shore. Now that, surely, would be an angling ultimate.

LURKING WITH INTENT The tarpon's languid appearance belies a most frightening turn of speed, making it a highly prized angling adversary. Our guide, Graeme, floated out his pinfish live bait, but it was a while before one of the fish showed interest. Graeme tried his best to hold my first-ever tarpon for a picture, but fish this size do not like posing.

TACKLE & TECHNIQUES

The methods used when fishing for sharks and tarpon are diametrically opposed. Sharks will come looking for you if you put out enough chum, but if you want to catch tarpon, there is no alternative but to go looking for them.

For sharks, we would head for likely areas, anchor in very shallow water, and then put out chum until they turned up. Sharks are free-swimming fish, and basically we were offering them what they wanted. Chum can be had ready-made in net-type bags, and we also bought bonito and dorado carcasses from the bigger charter vessels and hung those over the side. The resulting oily slick also attracted many of the pinfish that we used for live bait.

Although there is some tide in the Florida flats, the weight of the wire trace was sufficient to take a bait down to the bottom of the shallow water and hold it there. We would lob the live bait away from the boat and a short distance downtide so that it rested away from us and right in the middle of the chum.

To find tarpon, you need good local knowledge, which in Florida is provided by professional guides. Once you have found your fish, the actual fishing could not be simpler. You drift or anchor up, depending on where you are fishing, and let your live bait move downtide under a cork float until, hopefully, it is intercepted. Then comes the hard part, which is to hold on to a big fish that is desperately trying to shake the hook.

One gratifying thing in Florida is that the tarpon are never killed; having been brought to the side of the boat, their weights are estimated and then they are all unhooked and released.

CHUM *(below left)* Smelly, oily ingredients, such as blood and chopped fish, attract the predators.

PINFISH *(below)* A beautifully marked pinfish—the favored bait for shark and big tarpon.

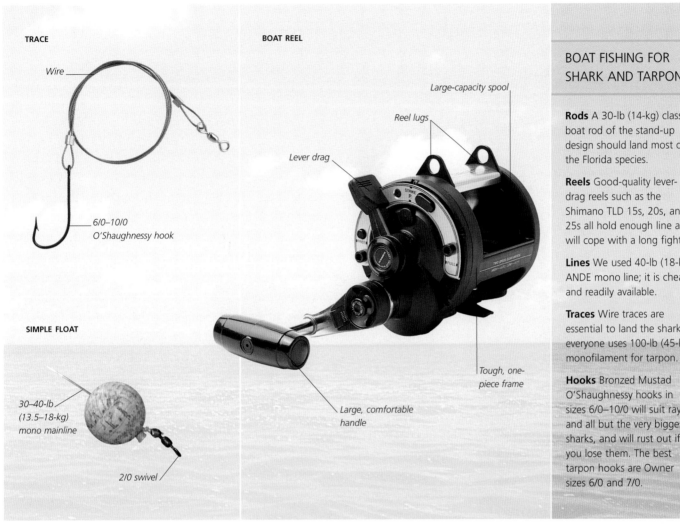

TRACE

Wire

6/0–10/0
O'Shaughnessy hook

SIMPLE FLOAT

30–40-lb
(13.5–18-kg)
mono mainline

2/0 swivel

BOAT REEL

Large-capacity spool

Reel lugs

Lever drag

Tough, one-piece frame

Large, comfortable handle

BOAT FISHING FOR SHARK AND TARPON

Rods A 30-lb (14-kg) class boat rod of the stand-up design should land most of the Florida species.

Reels Good-quality lever-drag reels such as the Shimano TLD 15s, 20s, and 25s all hold enough line and will cope with a long fight.

Lines We used 40-lb (18-kg) ANDE mono line; it is cheap and readily available.

Traces Wire traces are essential to land the sharks; everyone uses 100-lb (45-kg) monofilament for tarpon.

Hooks Bronzed Mustad O'Shaughnessy hooks in sizes 6/0–10/0 will suit rays and all but the very biggest sharks, and will rust out if you lose them. The best tarpon hooks are Owner sizes 6/0 and 7/0.

LIVEBAITING *(below)* A spherical cork float anchors the live bait just where you want it in the water.

CAUGHT OUT *(below)* This large nurse shark has fallen for our hefty fish bait and is finally being brought alongside the boat.

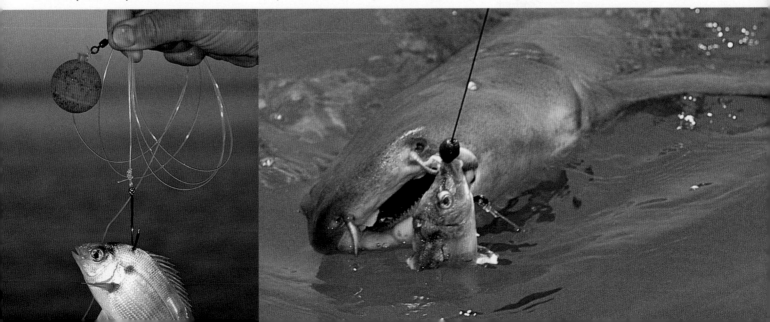

BRITISH OFFSHORE WRECK FISHING FOR POLLACK

The prospect of taking a boat far out into the English Channel and fishing over the rusting hulks of sunken ships is one to stir any angler's soul. But why do it? A wreck is a haven for fish; a boat goes down, and this provides shelter within perhaps a barren area of sand and mud. Various organisms soon find the structure, then small fish come along and graze on them; eventually these attract predatory fish such as conger eel, ling, pollack, cod, and coalfish. The big fish lurk around the structure, sheltering from the tide and feeding when the time is right. In time the wreck becomes a kind of oasis on the previously empty seabed.

Finding wrecks and fishing over them has been made far easier by the arrival of the GPS (Global Positioning System) and a formidable array of electronic equipment. But drifting and anchoring over wrecks requires skills that no machine can provide. Wreck fishing is a precise and demanding sport—drift or anchor in the wrong places and you have no success at all. That is why I always fish with professional skippers—they know what they are doing.

THE ENVIRONMENT

Wreck fishing in the English Channel is offered by specialized boat companies operating out of most of the ports on the English south coast. Most of the wrecks are vessels sunk during World War I and II, although warfare and foul weather claimed many more in earlier centuries. The Channel contains more wrecks per square mile than anywhere else on earth.

Temperatures in January average at about 36°F (2°C) in the east of the Channel, warming to 41°F (5°C) off Cornwall in the west. The strongest winds usually occur in late fall and winter, but gales are also experienced in summer.

Rainfall and sunshine The wettest months on the English Channel, which are also the least sunny, are November, December, and January. The weather is driest in April, May, and July, although on average May, July, and August offer the most hours of sunshine.

Key fish include pollack, conger eel—100 lb (45 kg) is not unheard of—ling, lunker cod, and coalfish.

Other fish include black bream, pouting, whiting, and bass.

Prime time for conger is during the summer, while there are two distinct runs of pollack, during summer and winter. Winter fish are preparing to spawn, and they are bigger and faster.

"If a pollack hits your bait, about the worst thing you can do is strike..."

Very early on a bitingly cold, late February morning, skipper Jim O'Donnell cleared the breakwater at Plymouth, England, and turned his boat, the *Tiburon*, on a southeasterly course toward a cluster of wrecks 30 miles (50 km) away. On board the 35-ft (10-m) vessel, a group of anglers that included myself were buzzing at the thought of the big pollack that had been feeding all winter at the wrecks and would soon be leaving to spawn. Winter wrecking on the English Channel is only possible during breaks in the weather, so we were feeling very lucky to be going fishing.

Arriving at our mark, the engines were throttled back and we got into our positions on the deck, ready for the first drift. Jim let

the boat run over the wreck to ascertain how the tide and breeze would push the vessel, then steered back uptide to set a perfect fishing drift. Once more the engine quieted to idle. Jim shouted every wreck fisherman's favorite phrase, "Down you go, boys!," and away to the depths streamed everybody's gear. All was quiet as the engine purred and 10 sets of tackle headed toward the huge, silent mass of ironmongery some 260 ft (80 m) below.

The first bites

Stop the reel as the lead hits the bottom, quickly wind up 10 turns, and then start the steady retrieve of the rubber lures; 10 of us concentrated hard on nothing but winding up perhaps a further 50 turns, and then repeating the process. There is nothing hugely technical about the angling side of wreck fishing, but you must have perfect control over both the clutch and your natural desire to strike a biting fish. If a pollack hits your bait, about the worst thing you can do is strike; it is absolutely essential just to keep winding and let the fish take the lure at its own pace. You will know when a pollack is on—it will arch over the rod and then go into a spectacular crash-dive. We had no takes on the first drift, but on the second Steve shouted out as a fish took the bait and dived; then others of us hooked up.

LURED OUT The net is placed under a good-sized, lure-caught pollack. The lures must be worked hard, and fish seem to prefer particular speeds on different days.

ALTERNATIVE
LOCATIONS

Wrecking is mainly a British fishing specialty—with so many wrecks in British waters, skippers have developed the skills to fish them. But wherever you are, fish tend to hang around sunken features, whether they be wrecks, reefs, sandbanks, oil rigs, or tidal rips. Wrecking works on a simple principle: go to where the fish congregate and you will find predators.

Netherlands

A few Dutch skippers head out into the southern waters of the North Sea and fish the wartime wrecks for huge cod and ling. This kind of fishing seems to be growing in popularity. Settled weather is of the utmost importance in wreck fishing because the boats often head a long way offshore in search of sport.

Denmark

Some Danish skippers specialize in reef fishing and head for the famous Yellow Reef system. Reef fishing is not unlike wreck fishing. The Danes fish for cod with large pirks; by all accounts they land some enormous fish—cod of over 50 lb (23 kg) are not uncommon.

Sweden

Sunken islands in Swedish waters were, I discovered, prime places to look for pike. Just as a deepwater wreck holds stocks of bait fish and attracts big predators, so the Swedish pike congregate around these underwater features and prey on the small fish swimming around them.

"We all lost our fish as they dived and hit the wreck's bridge, snagging our lines..."

The fast tide was pushing us past the wreck at some speed, so our drifts had to be short. Two 10-lb (4.5-kg) pollack came over the side, but things did not seem to want to get any busier on the next few drifts. Feeling that perhaps the tide was a little too strong, Jim decided to take us 10 miles (16 km) farther out to the wreck of the *Murree*, where he thought that the ebbing tide would work in our favor. Pollack love tide, but if it is too fast they tend to look for shelter and stop feeding.

The freighter *Murree* sank in 1989. A massive structure that looms menacingly on the echo sounder, it offers fish shelter from the tide and affords the pollack rich pickings of bait fish such as scad and herring. The ship's bridge projects some 100 ft (30 m) from the bottom. Although it is a magnet for anglers' tackle, you have to weigh the potential for fantastic sport against the risk of losing gear.

Approaching the *Murree*, we found that three other boats obviously had had exactly the same idea as our skipper and were already drifting and catching fish. Jim lined up the *Tiburon* once more, and again our gear went down, chasing prime winter pollack.

Pollack in the net

After perhaps 20 turns of the reel from the bottom, I felt a familiar pluck at the rod tip. Trying to control my instinct to strike, I simply kept winding, hoping that the fish would take. Another five turns of the handle and the rod slammed over, tip in the water, and line started to stream from the reel against the clutch. You can't help but smile when a pollack hits, but the smile is soon replaced by a little anxious twitch as you will the fish to

stop diving before it reaches the sanctuary of the wreck. My fish turned; I started to take in a little line, then the tip went over again and out went more line. You have to set the drag correctly and keep fighting the fish, but then it is usually yours. I looked over the side to catch the flash of white as the sun hit the pollack's flank, and then stood back to let Jim net my fish. At about 14 lb (6.5 kg) it was not going to threaten any records, but it was a typical, plump, winter fish. Get one over the 16-lb (7-kg) mark and you are a lucky angler; some fish over 20 lb (9 kg) are landed most winters, but that is an exceptional weight.

Hooked but lost

As the tide turned, we began to hook what must have been larger specimens, but we all lost our fish as they dived and hit the wreck's bridge, snagging our lines. You can't do much about that except utter a quiet curse and hope it doesn't happen again. But it always will, for this is pollack fishing as it is meant to be. Maybe fishing live launce for pollack over the reefs in spring is better still, but that is a different kind of fishing altogether.

Eventually it was time to turn and head for home, so we settled down and talked over the day and the fish we had landed; perhaps our best fish was a shade over 17 lb (7.7 kg). As the sun dipped below the horizon and the temperature dropped, all too soon our trip was over and the *Tiburon* back at her moorings in Plymouth. Strong winds were forecast for the following afternoon. Who could know when it would next be possible to head out into the English Channel and try to plunder its wrecks for prime, hard-fighting, winter pollack?

HIDDEN DEPTHS Under an overcast winter's sky, we dropped our lures from the drifting boat onto the wreck lying invisible below. The arc of one rod clearly indicates that a pollack is desperately diving to the bottom in a bid to escape the net. My pollack was no record-breaking fish, but just having lured it from its ghostly lair was satisfaction enough.

TACKLE & TECHNIQUES

The rig that is most effective for pollack, coalfish, and, to a lesser extent, cod is called "the flying collar." This consists of 13 ft (4 m) or more of 30-lb (14-kg) clear trace attached to a long wire boom, which keeps the trace clear of the mainline. The lure, together with leads of 6–14 oz (170–400 g), is tied to the end of the trace.

The flying collar rig is simply sent to the bottom, then retrieved at a steady rate. When you feel a hit from a pollack, it is essential to keep winding until the rod hoops over; resist the strong urge to strike, or you will miss the fish. You must set your reel's drag firmly enough to prevent it from reaching the snags among the wreckage, but not so firmly that the fish can snap the mainline.

For pollack, coalfish, and cod, try redgills, Eddystone eels, jelly worms, and shads, varying the shapes and colors. Fresh mackerel, squid, and cuttlefish are successful bait for conger and ling.

For conger, the skipper anchors his boat so that your lines run back in the tide to finish in the most promising fishing area. Simple running-ledger rigs are baited up and then dropped to the seabed, taken to the bottom by a hefty lead weight. Conger bait can also attract scavenging ling, as well as big cod. The secret of success is to keep the bait hard to the bottom, even when a swell is moving the boat up and down. Bites range from extremely timid (big conger often bite like this) to the typical knock–knock sensation caused by ling.

GOOD GEAR The flying collar rig (below left) and heavy-duty wrecking equipment (bottom left).

IN ALL COLORS (below) No rubber or plastic lure works every time, so keep a good selection.

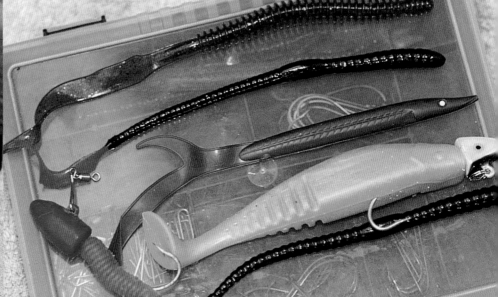

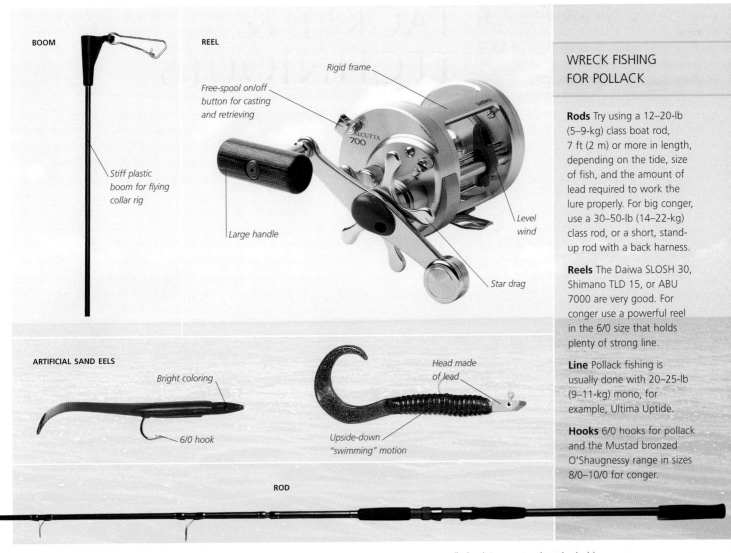

BOOM

Stiff plastic boom for flying collar rig

REEL

Rigid frame

Free-spool on/off button for casting and retrieving

ALCUTTA 700

Large handle

Level wind

Star drag

ARTIFICIAL SAND EELS

Bright coloring

6/0 hook

Head made of lead

Upside-down "swimming" motion

ROD

WRECK FISHING FOR POLLACK

Rods Try using a 12–20-lb (5–9-kg) class boat rod, 7 ft (2 m) or more in length, depending on the tide, size of fish, and the amount of lead required to work the lure properly. For big conger, use a 30–50-lb (14–22-kg) class rod, or a short, stand-up rod with a back harness.

Reels The Daiwa SLOSH 30, Shimano TLD 15, or ABU 7000 are very good. For conger use a powerful reel in the 6/0 size that holds plenty of strong line.

Line Pollack fishing is usually done with 20–25-lb (9–11-kg) mono, for example, Ultima Uptide.

Hooks 6/0 hooks for pollack and the Mustad bronzed O'Shaugnessy range in sizes 8/0–10/0 for conger.

SEIZED OPPORTUNITY *(below)* Use 200-lb (90-kg) mono for ling—they have very sharp teeth.

HEFTY FISH *(below)* A contented angler holds a prime wreck-caught pollack for the camera.

TROLLING FOR SALMON OFF CANADA'S PACIFIC COAST

Is it really possible to charter a boat, head out into the sea, and catch maybe 50 prime salmon? That was the question going through my mind as as we finally pulled into the tiny village of Bamfield, lying on the southern shore of Barkley Sound, on the west coast of Vancouver Island. All the way there I had silently prayed that our destination would live up to my expectations, and the place and view was everything that I could have imagined—a breathtaking vista of densely wooded mountains plunging down into deep blue water.

Outside our simple fishing lodge lay the vast expanse of the mighty Pacific, and that was where we hoped to find some salmon and halibut. The whole place seemed to live and breathe recreational fishing, and everybody we spoke to either owned a boat or was just going out fishing with friends. You do not witness those levels of excitement unless there is some good fishing to be had. Vancouver Island has lots of fish, but it also knows how to manage its resources and bring real revenue into the local economy. Anglers are welcomed and keep coming back, not only because of the fishing but because they are catered to extremely well.

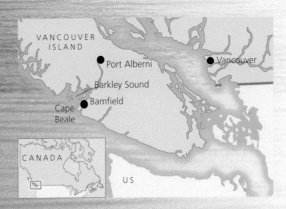

"It is out there that the huge shoals of migrating salmon hole up and feed..."

SALMON IN ABUNDANCE The Canadian Pacific Ocean has huge stocks of competing salmon species—which simply offers more choice for the angler.

Leaving Bamfield's little Grappler Inlet at 6 am, our skipper, Larry Charles, turned his 28-ft (8.5-m) boat toward the rolling swell of the Pacific Ocean and opened up the throttles. Soon we were bracing ourselves as the boat started punching into the heavy swell at over 25 knots. Our destination was a huge offshore bank situated 28 miles (45 km) west of Cape Beale. It is out there that the huge shoals of migrating salmon hole up and feed, and we were also hoping to see some halibut.

Trolling over the sandbank

Once we were over the bank, which lay 210 ft (64 m) below us, Larry turned off the main engine and set up the small four-stroke outboard to troll our lures underwater at a very slow and constant speed. We brought out the longer, softer downrigging rods and attached the lures to the line clips. Larry wanted to get our lures down to the big spring salmon at around 180 ft (55 m). The first lure was sent down via the right-hand downrigger, then it suddenly popped out and the rod sprang back. We had a fish.

Hardly believing that something could be on the end that quickly, I grabbed the rod as line began to run off the reel. Soft rods bend in the most alarming way, but they act as a cushion to crash-diving fish. After pumping the rod for over five minutes, I got my coho salmon to within netting distance.

THE ENVIRONMENT

Vancouver Island offers an ideal base for Pacific Ocean fishing trips. The waters teem with large fish, some of them migrating to rivers of the Canadian west coast to spawn, others moving between feeding grounds. Successive waves of species passing through the waters ensure excellent fishing year-round.

Temperatures on the ocean are governed by prevailing westerly winds. The average temperature in summer is 57°F (14°C); in winter the average temperature falls to 43°F (6°C).

Rainfall and sunshine The west coast of Vancouver Island has more than 130 in (300 cm) of rain annually. Conditions are dryer at sea, away from the mountainous coast. Sunshine is highly variable, and there can be heavy cloud cover in winter.

Key fish include chinook, coho, pink, sockeye, and chum salmon; halibut; and sea trout. Early chinook salmon reach weights of 40–60 lb (18–27 kg); the coho grows to more than 20 lb (9 kg). Halibut of over 150 lb (68 kg) are caught.

Other fish include ling cod and red snapper.

Prime time for the fishing varies greatly according to where you fish. Broadly, for chinook and coho salmon, try in August and September. Halibut is best sought between February and April. Steelhead trout tend to be most plentiful between December and February.

OCEAN SALMON We used light, flexible rods and downriggers to get lures down to the salmon beneath us. When trolling lures, I would normally expect to wait for a take, but here the coho were on to them instantly. My perfect coho specimen was just one of many that struggled valiantly against the hook.

"Salmon after salmon fought furiously all the way to the net..."

The coho weighed over 10 lb (4.5 kg); it was all I could do to wipe the big smile from my face. Then, for the next two hours, we tried hard to get lures down to the spring salmon swimming at deeper levels, but our efforts were in vain. Almost every time we tried, a coho closer to the surface would grab the lure on the way down, or rip the whole end rig from the tight clutches of the line clip.

It became one of those action-packed sessions that normally you only dream about. Salmon after salmon fought furiously all the way to the net, to be released unharmed—especially easy since by law we were using barbless hooks. Fish from 5–20 lb (2–9 kg) kept us on our toes and manically busy. Really, for us visiting anglers, it made no difference that the spring salmon were being beaten to the lures every time by the voracious cohos.

Trying for halibut

While we were battling with the cohos we were aware that below us there could also be halibut, and we were all desperate to see one. The west coast of Canada is famous for its high-quality halibut fishing, and in most weeks of the season a fish of 100 lb (45 kg) or more is brought to the scales at our lodge. We were right at the tail end of the main run of fish and knew that we would need some luck to get our lures among the giant flounders.

Keeping to the same trolling speed and staying on the same grounds, we brought in our salmon rods and sent the heavier halibut gear over the side. Within perhaps 10 minutes, our left-hand rod suddenly slammed over.

LATE-SEASON HALIBUT These fish can grow to an impressive size, and you need to use heavy line in case a monster takes your lure. You can see how my guide, Graeme, is leaning back to bring in his fish, yet his hard-won catch is only a fraction of the size of the biggest, fully grown specimens in Canadian waters. It was still a good-sized fish for late in the season.

"The real giants can be extremely dangerous when brought to the side of the boat..."

It was the turn of our fellow angler, Peter Scott, to strike, so he picked up the rod, waited until the unseen fish really tried to move off, and then set the hooks. Instantly the powerful rod arched over: battle had commenced. Peter was faced with the long haul to get the fish to the boat. Although before long we could tell that this was no monster fish, Larry said that it could only be one thing: a halibut.

Our guide, Graeme Pullen, and I were looking over the side to see the fish coming up from the depths, when suddenly Larry swung with the gaff and lifted a halibut over the gunnels. This looked like a fairly big fish to me, but in reality it was around 20 lb (9 kg), referred to as a "chicken" by the locals; the real giants can be extremely dangerous when brought to the side of the boat, and are handled with great care. Graeme later caught a 25-lb (11-kg) "chicken," after which things went quiet, so unfortunately I never got a chance to land a halibut myself.

Independent inshore fishing

After another day of salmon fishing over the bank, we rented boats from our lodge owner and went to troll some inshore waters much closer to home, in Grappler Inlet and along a well-known local mark known as the Wall. Very deep water lay extremely close to the wooded shoreline, and pockets of salmon were patrolling up and down as they approached the mouths of the rivers they swim up to spawn.

The fishing was quieter than offshore in terms of fish caught, but it was very enjoyable to take out a boat and do things yourself. Obviously we could not go offshore in small boats, but this kind of inshore work is safe,

relatively easy to do, and there are plenty of good fish to be had. The Wall is no more than a two-minute run in the boat from Bamfield, so you are never far from home. Exactly where you can fish is governed by strictly enforced local regulations. The goal is sustainable fishing for all, and for that fish need to be protected at certain times and in various locations.

For the inshore trolling, we made use of the downriggers, setting them up to fish with our own rods and reels. Then it was a case of slow trolling and waiting until the line suddenly jumped free from the clip. As fast as you can, you wind down until you make contact with the salmon—that is when the fun begins. While I did see a few big spring salmon landed by other boats, most of the fish caught were the more common coho salmon. Coho certainly fight, but when I finally hooked a 20-lb (9-kg) spring, it was a different story.

Encounter with a spring salmon

Early one morning we were trolling around a very deep ledge just off the Wall, with only bald eagles soaring above and the gentle purr of a slow-running outboard for company. My line suddenly ripped out of the clip and the tip did not spring back but instead stayed down. As usual it was a mad dash to grab the rod from the downrigger's clutches and start to fight the fish. Right away it was obvious that this was a slightly different fish, since it ran and ran—still, I set the clutch and had every hope that I would land it. But as the spring came to the net, it seemed to look at me, disliked what it saw, and promptly spat out the hooks. The spring would have been released anyway, but I was sorry not to get a trophy photograph.

TACKLE & TECHNIQUES

On Vancouver Island, all the boats used for fishing have downriggers attached to their gunnels. Downriggers are essential for deep trolling for salmon, where the lure or bait must be carried down to depths of 200 ft (60 m) or more.

A downrigger consists of a winder and an arm that projects from the boat. Via the arm, the winder lets out or takes in a wire line to which is attached a lead ball weighing 10 lb (4.5 kg) or more. On bigger boats the winder can be activated by the flick of a switch; on smaller boats it is cranked manually.

The angler's rod is placed in a holder and the mainline, with its rigged bait or lure, is attached by a clip to the wire, next to the ball. The ball and attached lure are then let down to where the fish

are swimming. The heavy weight on the downrigger ensures that the light lure is being trolled at the desired depth. With the lure trolling below, the line is then reeled in tightly so that the rod tip bends right over. A rod with a soft action is essential because a stiff rod would simply pull the line out of the clip every time the line was reeled in.

When a fish takes the lure, the force of the bite rips the mainline from the clip and you are left to fight the fish without hindrance from the weight.

Most local anglers use big flasher boards above the trace to the lure; these are reflective plastic boards that rotate when the lure is trolled. Their job is to attract the salmon to the lure, and they do their work extremely effectively.

INSHORE ACTION (*below*) Graeme holds onto a fly-caught salmon as it runs hard.

FIXED SPOOL (*below*) Your chosen fixed-spool reel must have a very smooth drag system.

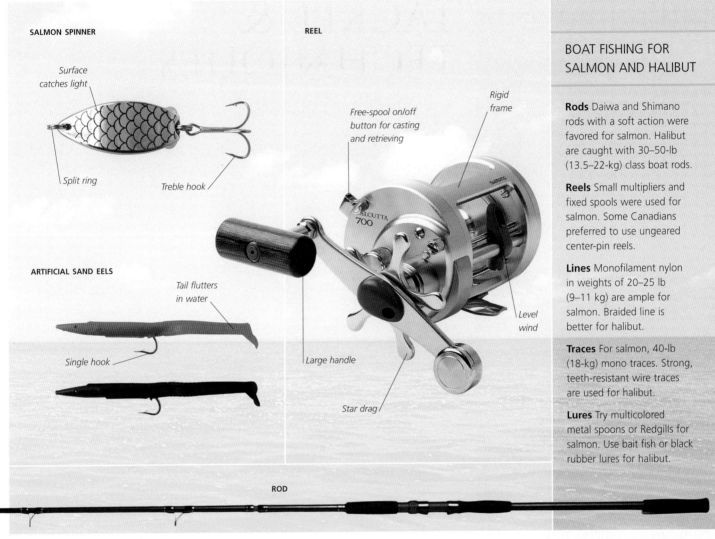

SALMON SPINNER

Surface catches light

Split ring

Treble hook

ARTIFICIAL SAND EELS

Tail flutters in water

Single hook

REEL

Free-spool on/off button for casting and retrieving

Rigid frame

Level wind

Large handle

Star drag

BOAT FISHING FOR SALMON AND HALIBUT

Rods Daiwa and Shimano rods with a soft action were favored for salmon. Halibut are caught with 30–50-lb (13.5–22-kg) class boat rods.

Reels Small multipliers and fixed spools were used for salmon. Some Canadians preferred to use ungeared center-pin reels.

Lines Monofilament nylon in weights of 20–25 lb (9–11 kg) are ample for salmon. Braided line is better for halibut.

Traces For salmon, 40-lb (18-kg) mono traces. Strong, teeth-resistant wire traces are used for halibut.

Lures Try multicolored metal spoons or Redgills for salmon. Use bait fish or black rubber lures for halibut.

ROD

SPARKLERS *(below)* These silvery flies were very effective when trolled behind the boat.

SPINNER *(below and bottom)* A spinner that works well for salmon in fresh water will do equally well in the sea.

TROLLED FLY *(below)* Graeme's salmon took a fly trolled behind the boat.

FISHING FOR PORBEAGLE SHARKS IN ENGLAND

The porbeagle shark comes from the same family as the great white and the mako, and looks like a smaller cross between the two. Being a mackerel shark, it likes to skulk around rocks and reefs and ride on the tide to snatch its prey. Porbeagles can be taken from Welsh waters, off the northern tip of Scotland, and off the Isle of Wight, but to me the spiritual home of these fish will always be the waters off the beautiful but treacherous north Cornish coast. It was there that the former world record for a porbeagle, 465 lb (211 kg), was hooked.

Most porbeagle fishing takes place from the towns of Padstow, Rock, and Bude—indeed, the shark's unusual name may derive from the Cornish term "porghbugel," meaning "port of Bude." The heyday of the fishing occurred in the 1970s and 1980s, when a flotilla of boats would leave the towns to enjoy spectacular sport on the shark's grounds off Bude and Crackington Haven. Far fewer skippers now chase the porgies, but one Padstow-based skipper still offers anglers a chance of hooking one of the true big game fish of Great Britain.

It was an early summer's morning in the Cornish seaside town of Padstow. Phil Britts, our skipper, untied the ropes and we slowly motored away from the quay, while Mike Turner, his crew and co-owner of the boat, tidied away fenders and buoys. We were aboard *Blue Fox* and riding north with the rugged Cornish coast on our starboard side. But when the engines slowed, I could not help but think that Phil was off-course, for our boat was lying less than 300 yd (275 m) from the rocky shoreline. I was fully expecting to head out into open water, but, thinking about it, fishing tight to the shore made perfect sense. While blue sharks wander the oceans and never seem to come close to the shore (except for some very deep areas), the porgie haunts relatively shallow, rocky, reefy places where the tide flows strong; our position, in grounds lying off Crackington Haven, was ideal.

Phil had a chart marked with the position of every porbeagle that had been hooked or seen from his various boats. The marks formed distinct clusters in certain areas, and clearly the large majority of shark action had taken place within 2 miles (3 km) of the shore.

POINTED LOOK Large and small porbeagle alike have a fearsome array of teeth. Somehow they seem to pose for the camera in the most menacing, threatening way.

"Thinking about it, fishing tight to the shore made perfect sense..."

THE ENVIRONMENT

North Cornwall is probably still one of the best places in Britain to fish for porbeagle sharks. The area is famous for its sharks off Bude and Crackington Haven.

Temperatures in the winter are comparable to those in Mediterranean resorts at the same time, rarely falling below freezing point. The average temperature in summer is 65°F (18°C).

Rainfall and sunshine Lightweight rain clothes are usually needed in Cornish waters, since the weather is notoriously unpredictable. Average rainfall per year is heavy at 34 in (863 mm); the annual sunshine average is over 1,500 hours.

Key fish in the waters off the north Cornish coast are porbeagle and blue sharks.

Other fish include pollack, tope, ling, conger eel, gurnard, huss, rays, bream, cod, whiting, and mackerel. Wrasse and bass are taken closer inshore.

Prime time for the bigger porbeagles is April and May, although they are fished successfully nearly year-round. Blue sharks appear later, around early June.

ALTERNATIVE
LOCATIONS

Ireland
Everywhere on the Irish west coast there are boats drifting in very tight to the shore, mainly looking for blue shark. These come in so tight because the water is deep and there are ample bait fish shoals. Porbeagle sharks frequent the west as well, but they are not targeted by many people.

Florida
There are huge hammerhead and tiger sharks not very far offshore from the Keys, but for some reason not many of the local skippers like to target them.

South Africa
How can I talk about shark fishing and not mention the great white shark? A boat operating from Strauss Bay has a license to fish for them. All great whites caught from the boat must be returned to the water.

"We suddenly saw at least three sharks twisting and turning right off the stern..."

With Phil allowing the tide and wind to take the vessel slowly away from the shore, we emptied sacks of chum or "rubby dubby" (mashed up mackerel, oil, and bran) over the side. Before long, we hoped, sharks would sense this drifting, strong-smelling trail of chum and move on up to where the scent was strongest—which was, of course, the boat. On the way they would meet our mackerel bait, suspended from various floats.

It was more than a little eerie and strange, sitting there and waiting. We were drifting in silence, with a scent trail reaching out and insidiously drawing the sharks to our hooks, bringing the predator to the hunter. The tension was not diminished by our memory of seeing, a few years before, a great white shark passing through those exact same grounds. Did we really want to attract perhaps the ocean's most feared predators so close as to be literally beneath our feet? Certainly we did.

Fulfillment of a dream
Within half an hour, one of us hooked into the first porgie, albeit no monster. We raced to get the other rods out of the way of the action. While Phil worked at the reel, we suddenly saw at least three sharks twisting and turning right off the stern. Our skipper suddenly lunged forward, struck, and then handed me the rod. It was several moments before I fully comprehended that line was streaming away from the rod in my hands. Finally bringing myself back to the moment, I was fighting with my first porbeagle shark, and fulfilling a lifelong dream. I realized that the shark must have taken the mackerel bait just as Phil was winding it in to get it out of the way. Our

rubby dubby was clearly so potent that we had any number of hungry predators around us. I struggled to balance the pure elation of realizing a dream with the need to fight this thing properly, or at least in the best way I knew how, at the same time taking in some welcome advice from the boat's seasoned pros.

To fish or photograph?
All of a sudden, "my" shark charged in toward me. I thought I had lost it, for the line fell horribly slack, but under instruction I wound as fast as possible and made definite contact once more. I was just in time to see more than 100 lb (45 kg) of prime porbeagle shark, my dream fish, run straight at us and veer off up alongside the boat. In my eagerness to fix that perfect image in my mind, I momentarily forgot I was hooked up to the fish; it was not until line started to pour once more from the reel that I snapped back to reality.

After perhaps another 10 minutes, I handed the still-bucking rod to my brother, Julian. I find that I am increasingly happy to do this, because, although I fish, I take photographs as well and I needed some pictures. In my formative years I could never have given away a rod to somebody, even family, if there was still a fish pulling at the other end. But now, as angling has become my livelihood, fishing and photography seem to be complementary parts of the same sport. I knew I would get another chance to fight one of those magnificent creatures, and the look of shock on Julian's face as he fought his ferocious-looking adversary was a sight to behold. It was the same stunned, barely comprehending look that had been on my face only 15 minutes earlier.

DANGEROUS WATER Attracted by our chum slick, the first porbeagle shark appeared by the boat. My brother, Julian, was initially alarmed when I unexpectedly passed him my rod with a fighting shark on the end of the line. After the shark ceased to thrash in the water by the boat, Julian was able to display his 100-lb (45-kg) porgie.

TACKLE & TECHNIQUES

The first question facing the porbeagle shark angler is the weight of tackle that should be taken to sea. Not every fish will be of a monster size, so it may be tempting to use tackle in the 20-lb (9-kg) class. But porgies can fight too hard for their own good, and gear that is too light can allow the fish to harm themselves unnecessarily. Using heavier gear means that you can get the fish to the boat more quickly, and you are also better prepared for hooking a big shark. Experienced anglers use 30-lb (13.5-kg) class tackle, but a 50-lb (22.5-kg) class rod and reel is otherwise advisable.

Lines and traces

Mainlines of 40–50 lb (18–22.5 kg) are ample, but make sure you have a minimum of 350 yd (320 m) on the reel because porgies can run a long way in a short time. Fishing from a boat, the use of brightly colored line, such as the very strong and relatively cheap Ultima Seastrike in bright yellow, helps both you and the skipper to pinpoint the fish, and does not seem to put off sharks in any way. Traces must terminate in at least 3 ft (1 m) of stainless wire to withstand the sharks' sharp teeth. A length of perhaps 12 ft (3.6 m) of heavy mono rubbing leader is also required to resist wear on the line from the sharks' sandpaper-like skin.

To catch porbeagle sharks, mackerel bait is usually suspended at various depths and ranges on simple float rigs; small, plastic, soft-drink bottles make perfect floats. They need to hold the bait at a certain depth, and also must not provide too much resistance when a shark finds it. Often the only sign of the

CHUM (below left) Messily cut up, bloody mackerel proves an irresistible lure for sharks.

MACKEREL BAIT (below) Bait is prepared so that the hook is cleanly exposed and can do its job.

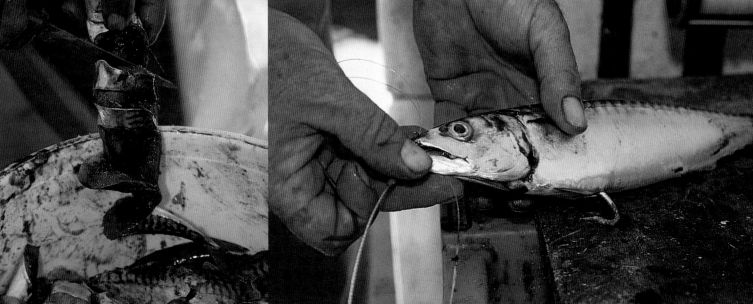

arrival of a shark is that the float flips over on its side; seagulls suddenly flying away from your chum slick also warn that sharks may be circling your bait.

Communication on the boat

Proper communication is always needed between angler, skipper, and crew. A skipper will always switch on the engine and "chase" a bigger fish, so keep your rod tip pointed at the fish and be ready to wind down fast. As well as using colored line as a visual aid in tracking the fish, it helps to leave your ratchet on. The ratchet's unmistakable sound gives the skipper more information about the fish's movements.

Unlike the blue shark, which likes open water, the porbeagle inhabits rough, snaggy ground. On the hook it can fight in a very "dirty" manner, tearing around just under the surface, then diving headfirst for the bottom. Keep up the pressure on a hooked fish, because you must try to prevent it from crash-diving for the nearest reef.

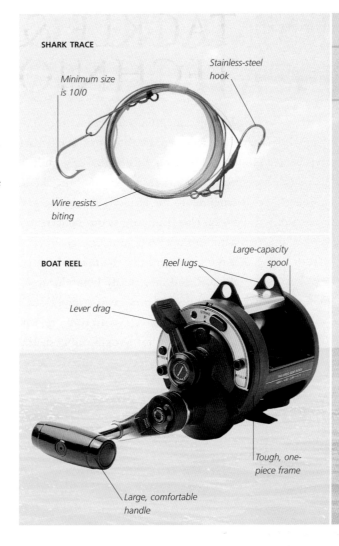

SHARK TRACE

Stainless-steel hook

Minimum size is 10/0

Wire resists biting

BOAT REEL

Large-capacity spool

Reel lugs

Lever drag

Tough, one-piece frame

Large, comfortable handle

BOAT FISHING FOR PORBEAGLE SHARKS

Rods The ideal is longer-than-normal boat rods in the 30-lb (13.5-kg) or 50-lb (22.5-kg) classes. First-timers would be advised to start off with the 50-lb (22.5-kg) gear.

Reels A large-capacity multiplier is essential, preferably with a smooth lever-drag system. Shimano, Okuma, and Penn all make good reels for this fishing.

Lines Mainline in the 40–50-lb (18–22.5-kg) class is perfect. Colored line indicates the direction of a fleeing shark. A wire trace is indispensable.

Hooks The Mustad Seamaster in 12/0 is very strong and is a popular but expensive pattern. Smaller, marlin-type hooks can be rigged in tandem as well.

BY THE BOAT *(below)* This could be your first glimpse of your catch.

POWERFUL MULTIPLIER *(below)* A hefty, lever-drag multiplier is the tool for successful porgie fishing.

REMOVING THE HOOK *(below)* Unhooking a shark is no job for a novice—those teeth are sharp.

THERE'S MORE TO FISHING THAN CATCHING FISH

Traveling the world and fishing places that I never expected to see was a tremendous privilege and pleasure. If this book inspires readers to collect their tackle together, jump on a plane, and visit some of the places I have described, or just one of them, it will have succeeded in its goal. Any angler who has crouched on the bank of a quiet river and enjoyed the thrill of outwitting a trout or barbel, or has hung on as an angry shark ripped yards of line from the reel, is glad to share those powerful experiences with like-minded people. To visit new locations and cast for unfamiliar species of fish is, for us anglers, the most interesting thing imaginable.

Catching tremendous trophy fish is the goal of every angler. There is a special, additional excitement in realizing that the fish on the end of your line is a magnificent specimen. Many anglers like to keep a record of their catches and for them the prime motivation is working to beat their personal best.

Quieter days on the water

Sometimes, the fish that come to the bait are not large, but you find yourself fighting several of them and you enjoy the sport. On other days, maybe only one fish is hooked. But how does the angler deal with a day when nothing at all is caught?

No truthful angler could ever say that fish never fail to come to the bait. Anglers are dealing with nature, and nature is the ultimate in unpredictability. If the fish are not there, or are simply not feeding on that day or night, then no skill on the part of the angler will make any difference to the outcome. On such days, I used to return home in a rage, vowing never to pick up a rod again, but the feeling does not last long; I acknowledge that nature has beaten me, fair and square.

Days that offer no catch are the days that bring fishing into perspective. We love to catch fish, but are we wasting our time if the day ends with nothing in the net? In my case, becoming a photographer has opened up a whole new dimension to the fishing experience. It just so happens that fishing takes all of us to many of the most beautiful parts of our world, and photography has taught me to appreciate the subtle qualities of landscape and the effects that the weather has on the light and the appearance of the sky. I am not suggesting that every angler should become a photographer; more that every angler can learn that catching fish is not the whole story of fishing. Just being aware of the environment, thinking about it and experiencing it consciously, is a wonderful source of pleasure in itself.

Experiencing perfection

To give an example, I had high expectations of the pristine fishing conditions on Vancouver Island. Cascading, pure water, snow-capped mountains, great forests, not a building in sight, and fine salmon rising to the lure. The reality was better than I had hoped, and I will never forget wading the Sarita River as each successive pool became more and more impressive and magical. Yet, on one day, there were huge fish in front of us and not one showed any interest in our bait. On occasions such as that, being able to take delight in the surroundings makes it perfectly possible to come away satisfied.

"Being aware of the environment, thinking about it and experiencing it consciously, is a wonderful source of pleasure in itself..."

INDEX

ACKNOWLEDGMENTS

Author's acknowledgments

There are so many people I would like to thank. Islay—for being my wife, putting up with my fishing, and for never hassling me to go and get a real job. Behind all that I do, you are there, providing strength, support, love, and encouragement; without you I would be lost. My parents—for giving me such a free and stable upbringing, and for always encouraging me and my two brothers to follow our hearts and minds in whatever we choose to do, even when we provide the odd moment of grief. My brothers—you will go a long way; have absolute faith in yourselves and never back down. My godmother, Lindy—she would have been so proud to see this book. My sheepdog, Jess, man's best friend—who else can I talk to when I am out fishing on my own?

Ian Whitelaw—for such tireless work on this book, and for your friendship; best of luck to you and the family. Mike Edwards—for being instrumental in getting this book started at DK; I am eternally grateful. Andrew Easton, Andy Ashdown, and Rob Beattie at Design Revolution— you did a wonderful job. Frank Ritter and Jo Grey—for coming in halfway through the project and providing such strong input. Dorling Kindersley— Stephanie Jackson, Nicki Lampon, Anna Benjamin, Derek Coombes, Adèle Hayward; this was a very exciting but fairly daunting project for me to take on, so thank you for keeping it on such a stable course for me, and for never questioning my ability to get the material.

Paul Martingell—my director/producer and a good friend; here is to the future and whatever it may bring. Steve McGuire—I might never have gone to Namibia if not for you, and for that I am forever grateful; the fishing is awesome. Graeme Pullen—for being so kind in getting me access to all that fishing and material in Florida and Canada. Mr. Holden and Mr. Somerset—two inspirational teachers who laid strong foundations in me at a very young age. John Bailey—for providing a young angler with so much inspiration and so much to aspire to; fishing and talking with you in Spain was a joy—you are a role model in angling today. Roger Mortimer—for fishing with me so tirelessly and generously in Florida. Phil Britts and Mike Turner—for being good friends and getting me access to the porbeagle sharks. The anglers of Plymouth, UK—for showing me nothing but kindness from my first day of living there. And to all the anglers I have met the world over—thank you for your generosity and help, and for allowing me to work my cameras right in the midst of your fishing.

I am also eternally indebted to my grandmother—she first took me fishing, and this lifelong obsession of mine was started by her. She was an awesome lady and the best grandmother in the world; I miss her very much, and I so wish that she could have seen this book.

Publisher's acknowledgments

Dorling Kindersley would like to thank the following for their contributions: Mike Edwards and Derek Coombes for their invaluable assistance, Anna Bedewell and Romaine Werblow for picture research, Margaret McCormack for the index, Patrick Mulrey for the maps, Ian Whitelaw and Design Revolution, and John Bailey.

Special thanks to the following for their help

The author gratefully acknowledges the help he received from the following individuals and companies in getting him to fishing locations and collecting material for this book.

Canada (salmon fishing, river and boat)
Murray Claughton, Box 68, Bamfield, B.C., Canada V0R 1B0
email: seabeamexico@hotmail.com

Canada (salmon fishing, river and boat) and Florida (boat fishing)
Graeme Pullen Fishing Holidays
tel/fax: 01252 615360

Florida (largemouth bass fishing)
Capt. A. James Jackson, AJ's Freelancer Bass Guide Service (Orlando)
tel:(407) 291 4555 or (800) 738 8144 (toll-free) email: CapJackson@aol.com
www.orlandobass.com

Ireland (pollack and thornback ray fishing)
Paul Harris (angling representative of the Irish Tourist Board), Loveitts Farm, Brinklow, Rugby, Warwickshire CV23 0LG tel: 01788 833203
email: paul@p-harris.demon.co.uk

Jersey (bass fishing)
Andrew Syvret tel: 01534 485201
email: pinnacle@localdial.com

Namibia (beach fishing for sharks)
MolaMola UK tel: 01284 762097
www.molamola.co.uk
Steve McGuire
    email: steve.mcguire@tiscali.co.uk

Spain (catfishing)
Dave McCoy, Millennium Fishing
tel: 0034 6678 54501
email: millenniumfishing@hotmail.com
www.catfishing.co.uk

Spain (barbel fishing)
John Bailey, In Wild Waters
tel: 07813 001632
email: enquire@inwildwaters.net

Sweden (pike fishing)
Anders Forsberg,
Västerviks Fishing Centre
email: info@vestervik.com
www.vestervik.com

UK (fly fishing)
Nick Hart (qualified guide and instructor)
tel: 01643 831101
email: nick@hartflyfishing.demon.co.uk
www.hartflyfishing.demon.co.uk

UK (porbeagle shark fishing)
Phil Britts, skipper of the Padstow-based boat, *Blue Fox*
tel: 01841 533293
mobile: 07977 563807

UK (wreck fishing)
Jim O'Donnell, skipper of the Plymouth-based boat, *Tiburon*
tel: 01752518811
email: jim@plymouthcharters.co.uk
www.plymouthcharters.co.uk

Picture acknowledgments

The publisher would like to thank the following for their kind permission to reproduce their photographs:

(Abbreviation: tl=top left.)

30–31: ImageState; **38:** ImageState (tl); **118–119:** N.H.P.A.; **128:** N.H.P.A. (tl); **134–135:** Getty Images/Harvey Lloyd; **142:** Getty Images/Harvey Lloyd (tl).

All other images © Henry Gilbey.

For further information see:
www.dkimages.com